KOMELIA HONGJA OKIM

Korean Metal Art

Techniques, Inspiration, and Traditions

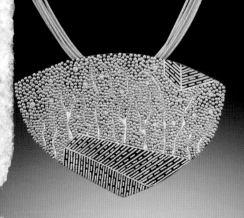

SCHIFFER PUBLISHING

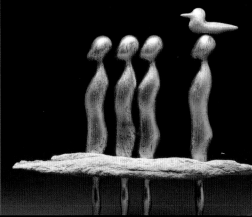

Other Schiffer Books on Related Subjects:

Cast: Art and Objects Made Using Humanity's Most Transformational Process, Jen Townsend and Renée Zettle-Sterling, ISBN 978-0-7643-5338-3

Narrative Jewelry: Tales from the Toolbox, Mark Fenn, Foreword by Jack Cunningham, PhD, ISBN 978-0-7643-5414-4

The author would like to acknowledge the following organizations for their grants in support of this project: The Fulbright Program providing the Korean-American Educational Commission (KAEC), the Hyosung Corporation, the Korea Arts Management Service (KAMS), and Gallery Sowyen.

Designed by Molly Shields
Cover design by Brenda McCallum
Type set in Credit Valley/Cambria

ISBN: 978-0-7643-5779-4
Printed in China

Published by Schiffer Publishing, Ltd.
4880 Lower Valley Road
Atglen, PA 19310
Phone: (610) 593-1777; Fax: (610) 593-2002
E-mail: Info@schifferbooks.com
Web: www.schifferbooks.com

For our complete selection of fine books on this and related subjects, please visit our website at www.schifferbooks.com. You may also write for a free catalog.

Schiffer Publishing's titles are available at special discounts for bulk purchases for sales promotions or premiums. Special editions, including personalized covers, corporate imprints, and excerpts, can be created in large quantities for special needs. For more information, contact the publisher.

We are always looking for people to write books on new and related subjects. If you have an idea for a book, please contact us at proposals@schifferbooks.com.

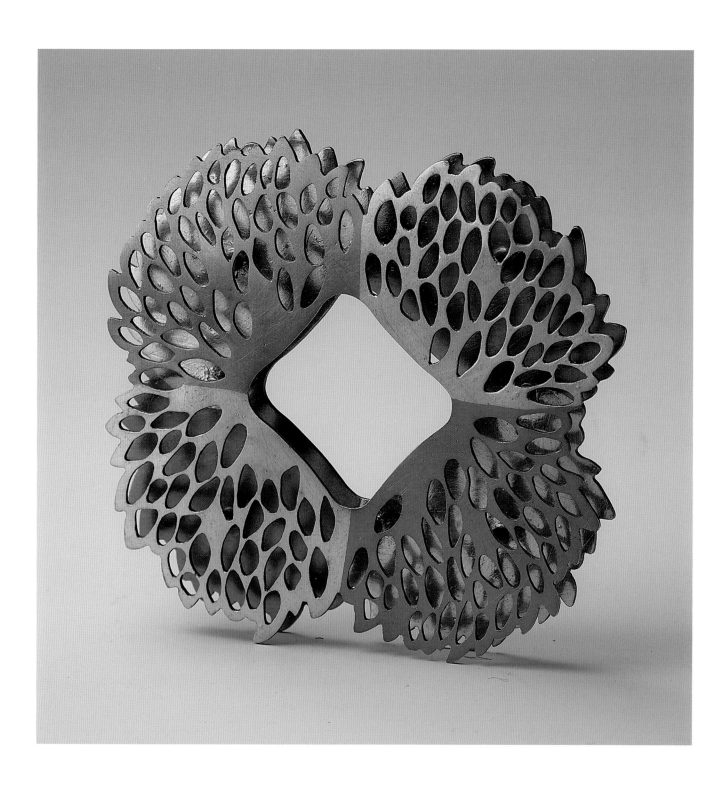

Contents

Foreword

Ms. Jai-Ok Shim, Executive Director of the Fulbright Korean-American Educational Commission

Dear Reader,

It is with highest regard that I write in support of Professor Komelia Hongja Okim's latest literary contribution, *Korean Metal Art*. I came to know Komelia in 1982, when she carried out her first Fulbright award in South Korea as a lecturer and researcher at Hong-ik University. Little did I know it then, but Komelia would return to Fulbright Korea again and again to refine her knowledge on Korean metal art (1994 at Won-Kwang University, 2015 at Gyeongju National Museum). As executive director of the Korean-American Educational Commission, I have met few people who possess as much curiosity as Komelia—and even fewer with the amount of drive she maintains to appease curiosity, to learn new information, and then to share knowledge with her community.

The Fulbright Program mission is to increase mutual understanding between the people of the United States and the people of other countries. Komelia has lived this mission for nearly half a century, not only in the United States and Korea, but worldwide. Her decision to write this book in English exemplifies her commitment to provide professionals and interested audiences from across the globe the opportunity to learn more of Korea's history of metalcraft and arts, which have been carried out for more than 5,000 years, and I am grateful her findings will continue to be shared through the foundations of educational and cultural exchange on which the Fulbright Program is built.

Komelia has expanded what the world knows about Korean metal art to an incredible extent, having quite literally saved centuries-old artifacts from being buried and forgotten any longer than they already had been. In so doing, she also unearthed Korean tradition that was unknown to the modern world prior to her efforts. And with each work of art discovered came a story. With each story recounted came culture. You will come to discover that Komelia has a true gift in bringing every piece of metal to life, giving every shrapnel a heart, and realizing every material's innate soul.

And so, it is my hope that once you close this book, a sense of the past will have settled in your mind, thereby allowing you to appreciate not only the fortunes you have in the present, but also those still waiting in your future. Art surrounds us; it's only a matter of how you decide to see it. Komelia decided long ago to see it in a very simple way . . . as existence.

JAI-OK SHIM
EXECUTIVE DIRECTOR, FULBRIGHT KOREAN-AMERICAN
EDUCATIONAL COMMISSION

Mr. Young-Hoon Yi, Former Director of Gyeongju National Museum and Former Director General of National Museum of Korea

I first met Professor Komelia Hongja Okim in June 2015, while I was serving as director of Gyeongju National Museum. A recipient of a research grant from the Fulbright Korean-American Education Commission, she worked for several months at Gyeongju National Museum as a visiting fellow.

Professor Okim presumably had various reasons to visit Gyeongju, an ancient city that served as the capital of the Silla Kingdom (57 BCE–918 CE) for nearly 1,000 years. Nevertheless, there is no doubt that her primary concern at the time was the unique gold culture of Silla, which is manifested in remarkable gold crowns. During her stay in Gyeongju, Professor Okim carried out her research on the museum's collection with great enthusiasm and visited with local metal craftspeople to exchange ideas on metal arts and crafts and learn more about their traditional techniques.

This book presents the results of Professor Okim's research and fieldwork in Korean metalcraft and related techniques. One of the primary strengths of this book lies in its wide-ranging discussion both on traditional and contemporary metal arts and crafts, on the basis of the author's extensive knowledge and experience as a contemporary metal artist. This publication is especially meaningful given that little has been written on the topic in English.

Examining the book, we are constantly reminded that the present is derived from the past. Just as a flower cannot leave behind its roots, artists create their works upon a foundation of what came before, and link us with the people in the past. This, I think, is one of the proper functions of art.

I hope readers will gain tremendous knowledge of the Korean metal arts and crafts as well as unique cultural backgrounds detected through these elaborate surface techniques seen through museum collections, government-designated crafts artists' replicas, and finally contemporary artists' works incorporating the traditional techniques and concepts in their contemporary expressions.

YOUNG-HOON YI
FORMER DIRECTOR, GYEONGJU NATIONAL MUSEUM
FORMER DIRECTOR GENERAL, NATIONAL MUSEUM OF KOREA

Acknowledgments

I would like to thank the Hyosung Corporation for financially supporting the creation of this book. Through the Korean-American Fulbright Senior Grant and the Institution of the Gyeongju National Museum, I was able to do very valuable research and perform close studies of Korean historical surface techniques. I would not have been able to complete this book without the funding of the Korean-American Educational Commission Scholarship of Korea, the Hyosung Corporation, the Korea Arts Management Service (KAMS), and the Gallery Sowyen of the Republic of Korea.

The last three years have been full of exciting and rewarding experiences as I collected more than 200 images from thirteen museums and individual collections. I owe a debt of gratitude to the directors, curators, and staff who assisted me in my research and sent me images to use for publication. I would like to especially thank the Gyeongju National Museum director, curator, and staff for allowing me to do intensive studies for more than two months.

My thanks also goes to the National Museum of Korea, the National Palace Museum, the Gongju National Museum, Ewha Womans University Museum, Sookmyung Women's University Museum, Seokjuseon Memorial Dankook University Museum, Baekbong Korean Traditional Jewelry Museum, the Lock Museum, and the Saekdong Museum, as well as being able to study the private collections of Cheonmisa (Daegu, Republic of Korea), Tokyo National Museum (Japan), and the Koryo Museum (Kyoto, Japan), and to the Museum of Fine Arts (Boston, USA) for their valuable historical images of Korean traditional surface-embellishing techniques.

Moreover, I am grateful to all the traditional craftspeople who have been carrying on the traditional crafts techniques, and to the 113 contributing metal artists from Korea, America, Canada, and Taiwan whose works are featured in this book.

I dedicate this book to my husband, Dr. Victor Eiichi Okim, who patiently supported me during the over two years I spent away from home, as well as the last three years I spent working on this book. Last but not least, I would also like to express my sincere appreciation and give thanks to my son and his wife, my siblings, and all my friends and professional colleagues who gave me moral support, immeasurable advice, and time in Korea, and in my home country, the United States.

Preface

As a Korean American metal art professor at Montgomery College for over forty-two years, I also taught numerous lectures and workshops at universities, craft schools, and metalcraft organizations across North America and around the world.

As I was in Korea teaching American metalsmithing techniques to students at Korean universities, I researched Korean metal arts techniques, which are similar to American metal arts techniques yet drastically unique in their patterns, themes, designs, technical usages, directions, and functions. I felt it was important for these Korean techniques to be introduced to American, English-speaking audiences, especially since I had lacked these valuable resources during my own metal arts studies in America.

While I was growing up in Korea and while studying fiber arts at Ewha Womans University, I knew nothing about metalsmithing and the art jewelry of Korea.

After moving to the United States at age twenty-one, I earned my BA and MFA degrees from Indiana University under the instruction of Professor Alma Eikerman. This broad base of knowledge in design, paintings, and sculptures as well as metal arts eventually helped introduce me to Korean university students and the exchange of metalsmithing techniques. While practicing and teaching metal arts and identifying my heritages, it became more important to me to discover and express my cultures and their art.

It is my sincere hope and desire to introduce and exchange the rich ideas, customs, and techniques of the Korean metal arts field to English-speaking artists, students, and collectors. There is much for us to learn and experience in Korean metal arts, techniques, and customs.

Introduction

Korean Traditional Metal Techniques, from Ancient to Contemporary

Traditional metalcraft related to every aspect of Korean customs, tradition, and daily life, as well as to important ceremonial events. Cooking pots, small portable iron charcoal burners, iron bowls and utensils for winter use, and brassware (and more recently stainless-steel) utensils for summer are found in almost every household today. Importantly, ceremonial and ritual functions continue to employ specially selected metalwares, in keeping with traditional customs. For example, brassware is used for ancestral memorial items exposed to weather, while silverware, due to its symbolism and value, is used for the special celebrations of the 100-day-old infant, the one-year-old child's birthday, and the sixtieth, seventieth, eightieth, and eighty-eighth birthdays.

Traditional wedding and engagement ceremonies in Korea were elaborate affairs, and common people with monetary wealth would spare no expense to follow the examples set by Korean royalty. Silver containers and utensils were usually employed and would be decorated with gold letters, patterns, and symbols designating good luck, happiness, blessing, or longevity. Gift giving on occasions such as these was and still is considered especially auspicious, with metalwares or 24K double-set gold rings or bracelets frequently offered. The child bracelet for the 100-day-old infant and the gifts for a one-year-old's birthday usually have jingling ornaments that add a note of playfulness to the occasion.

In third- or fourth-century usage, metal objects were usually reserved for use by the royal courts in religious ceremonies. The king, the queen, and government officials displayed their status through their ornamental jewelries and insignia. Warriors used specially constructed ornaments and amulets for protective purposes. All the objects possessed special meanings; each was decorated with symbolic designs and characters for protection, blessings, and longevity, shown through traditional character signs and floral/animal signs. These ornaments and ceremonial instruments were carefully designed and decorated by their makers, using elaborate embellishing techniques suited to each particular occasion and purpose. Further, the king's eating utensils were made in silver to detect potential poisons, since silver turns darker when it touches some poisons.

For centuries, Korea was called a hermit kingdom and was said to have little contact with its neighbors. In reality, before the fall of the Joseon dynasty in 1910, Korea was influenced by close relationships with several Chinese dynasties, Silk Road commerce, and some other neighboring countries. Imported Chinese techniques were incorporated by Korea's craftsmen and enhanced the metalwork used at royal courts, religious rituals, and ancestral-worship ceremonies. Metalcraft was so important for the royal courts that individual skilled craftsmen were designated and dedicated to serve the demands both of the courts and the upper-class families.

Korean craft production endured a dark period in the early years of the twentieth century, beginning with the Japan-Korean Treaty of 1910, which began the annexation of the Korean Empire by Imperial Japan. This annexation effectively ended the royal system of governance and patronage. Korean craftsmen were forcibly relocated to provide service for the government of Japan. Traditional language and culture were suppressed on the Korean peninsula. Only after the end both of World War II and the Korean War in the 1950s could the Korean government build a democratic system and establish a new modern governmental system—one that was changed from the old traditional royal system. Teaching and developing new crafts art and design courses at the college level began several years after the Korean War.

In 1962, the Korean government committed to preserving the nation's traditional cultural heritage, and toward this end it instituted the Korea Cultural Heritage Foundation (KCHF). This foundation is dedicated to preserve, protect, develop, enhance, and promote Korean "Intangible Cultural Properties." These are government-recognized skilled practitioners of the traditional crafts, designated to preserve the specialized techniques in their crafts areas. In this way, traditional and historical craft techniques continue and are handed down, propagated, and preserved. In metal arts, for example, TCHU Jeong-Ryeol received government support for his work; see his tobacco pipe in chapter 2.4.

In 2016, the official Intangible Cultural Properties title was refined into two categories: "National" and "Regional Province Designated." In both categories, the craftspeople are required to follow a process of application, screening, testing, and demonstrations administered by government-appointed committee members. The artisans who successfully pass the rigorous testing earn the title and are awarded a monthly stipend to support them in carrying on their special techniques and work. Indeed, as a consequence, many museum-held assets and historical artifacts that were damaged or lost between 1910 and the end of the Korean War are being restored or re-created by these master craftspeople in Korea today.

These masters can have assistants whom they train to continue their craft's unique techniques. The assistants and followers sit for examinations after three years of education and must undergo five years of apprenticeship before obtaining assistantships.

The Cultural Heritage Foundation (CHF) conducts special exhibitions for these craft artists. Some fairs invite masters of a craft and professional artists to relate their techniques to a contemporary idea or themed exhibition. These collaborative exhibitions have become increasingly popular since late 2000.

Because of the great popular interest in all crafts and craft arts in Korea today, many specialized shops have opened, as well as mixed-use craft shops and studios, especially in Seoul and other municipal areas. Art exhibitions are so popular that a new show is opened every week.

This book showcases and explains the Korean traditional metal surface embellishment techniques as seen through my museum research, direct observation of artifacts, and studio visits, with many designated as Intangible Cultural Properties (that is, living national treasures), as well as highlighting other metal artists.

There are eight chapters with twelve subchapters, examining different surface-embellishing techniques. Each chapter explains the origin of the specific techniques used and offers examples. Images of museum artifacts display examples of the technique, followed by the craftspeople's works, which include replicas and objects with traditional motifs, design, and techniques. The final portion of each chapter focuses on contemporary metal artists to show how they use or incorporate traditional techniques with contemporary metal techniques and concepts. For "modern contemporary" metal arts, I focus on works produced from 1980 through 2017.

Each chapter is organized into three main categories:

- MUSEUM COLLECTIONS, WITH HISTORICAL TECHNICAL REFERENCES

- CRAFTSPEOPLE, MAINLY FOCUSING ON HISTORICAL IMAGES/DESIGNS/ TECHNIQUES

- CONTEMPORARY ARTISTS WHO USE TRADITIONAL TECHNIQUES

Korean Symbolic Patterns Used on Objects and Wearable Ornaments

Traditionally, Koreans have employed images from nature to represent long life, wealth, happiness, health, good fortune and luck, integrity, honor, fidelity, and successful childbearing, especially of boys to carry on the family name. Craftsmen produced works with patterns related to these symbolic shapes and objects.

In Korean culture, *dragons* are brave, mythical animals that govern the rain and clouds. They symbolize nobility, authority, and the royal family. *Phoenixes* are mythical birds associated with Taoism. They symbolize goodness and mercy. During the nineteenth to twentieth centuries, the queen's clothing often took inspiration from phoenixes, incorporating the crane-like neck, golden feathers, and peacock-like tail into its designs. *Butterflies* stand for joy, happiness, and beautiful conjugal love. They are often used in *ddeoljam* (fluttering/trembling) accessories, the attention-commanding ornaments traditionally worn by kings and queens. *Bamboo* stands for integrity and fidelity. *Plum blossoms* were a messenger of springtime and good news. *Bats* were a popular Joseon-dynasty decorative-arts symbol. Bats bear many young, so they were considered a symbol of good fortune. They can also represent long or eternal life. *Chrysanthemums* are a type of flower that doesn't wither away but blooms in lofty solitude; therefore it is thought of as immortal. They and *peonies* are typical of Joseon decorative arts.

Mythical tigers, butterflies, bats, and *fish* are symbols to drive away evil spirits. *Scarecrows* symbolize prosperity of the family. *Eggplants, fish,* and *male figures* are popular motifs representing wishes to have many sons.

Arabesque and hieroglyphic patterns are used around animal and plant patterns to fill gaps between repeated units. *Plum flowers, bamboo, chrysanthemums, orchids, eggplants, peppers, peaches,* and *horned oranges,* as well as items such as *round vases, big drums, scarecrows,* and *boy figure patterns,* are expressions of wishes for the wealth and prosperity of the family and long life. *Chinese characters* stand for longevity, happiness, and health. Other popular patterns include perennial flowers such as *bell flowers,* and geometrical patterns such as *continuous steps and rails.*

Korean folding screens are a common gift at weddings and special occasions and are often decorated with the *ten longevity beings* of Korean culture: *sun, mountain, water, rocks, clouds, pines, elixir of life, turtle, crane, and deer.* The symbolic images convey wishes for long life and everlasting happiness.

CHAPTER 1

Cold Joining Techniques

Ax Cutting, Punch Decorating, Wire Connecting, and Dangling

Ax-cutting, punch-decorating, wire-connecting, and dangling techniques were used on pure gold, silver, and copper objects seen among the kings' ceremonial royal objects made by craftsmen during the third century in the Silla and Baekjae dynasties (37 BCE–1910 CE). This includes many decorative royal objects, such as wide open-work neck/shoulder ornaments, the kings' crowns, gold caps used for war ceremonies, and gold belts with pendants made of thin gold plates, complete with a buckle and belt strap end with hanging pendants.

On the gold belt shown here, thirteen pendants hang from a row of gold plates, which are heart shaped and decorated with a trefoil pattern that is based on the palmetto design. The open-work pattern is punched from the gold plates, and circular spangles are attached with twisted gold wires. Numerous pendants are assembled with chains of oval and rectangular plates. The longest chain consists of oval plates with three bells attached at the bottom.

Other charms that descend from this pendant include an acupuncture needle container, writing tablets, and a glass perfume bottle loosely encased with wire net. There is also a jade *gogok* in the shape of a question mark, which symbolizes both the seeds of life and hopes for rebirth. It is capped with a gold cup setting. Other charms include a fish, an open-work purse-shaped plaque, a gold *gogok*, a pair of open-work scissors, and a three-belled object. These objects exemplify the finest craftsmanship during the third and fourth centuries.

It is likely that the craftsmen worked with thin pure metals due to the limited availability and cost-effectiveness. This approach was necessary to add surface decorations of pointed dots and patterns by punching from the back, hammering the work with a dull-pointed metal tool set on a soft wood background. The process produced various ornamental objects and decorative open shapes from sharp cutting punches. Shapes were designed by punching open work with a sharp tool, rather than the saw that is typically used by contemporary metal artists. Craftsmen utilizing these techniques had to be extremely careful because the ornaments were delicate, made of the finest silver or gold. By punch-cutting the desired shapes and patterns, it was possible to create a variety of shapes. As the craftsmen continued to work the material, the punching techniques enhanced the design and the metal became work hardened. This allowed it to maintain its shape.

Decorative elements were not soldered but rather were connected by using very thin wires consisting of chains of jump-ring units or twisted wires used in hinging mechanisms. These dangling shapes and units made soft, subtle sounds and glittered as the king walked in ceremonial processions.

For effects echoing these historic treasures, contemporary artists use open works with punch-decorating patterns, wire works based on the historical techniques of punching patterns, open pierced designs, and dangling decorative units using wires.

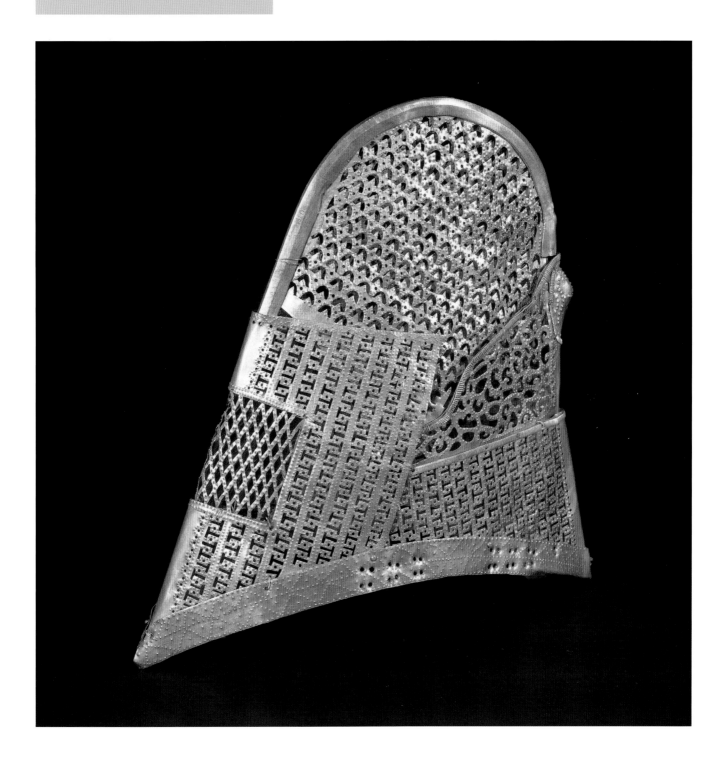

Gold Cap. NT No. 189. Silla dynasty,
sixth century. Open design with
gold wire and rivets (chisel cutting
and joinery). 7.5". *Gyeongju
National Museum*

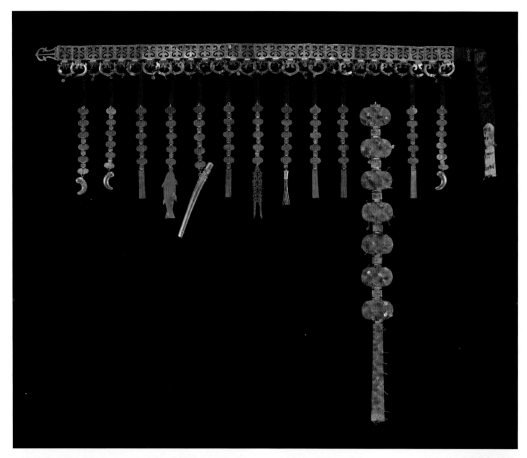

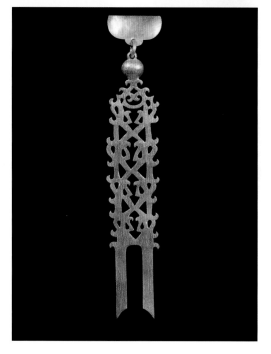

Gold Belt with 13 Hanging Pendant Ornaments. NT No. 192. Silla dynasty, fifth century. Pendant charms with an acupuncture needle container, writing tablets, a perfume bottle, a jade *gogok*, a fish, an open-work purse-shaped plaque, a gold *gogok*, a pair of open-work scissors, and a three-belled object. 42.9". *Gyeongju National Museum*

Gold Belt with 13 Hanging Pendant Ornaments. NT No. 192 (close-up). *Gyeongju National Museum*

Gold Belt with 13 Hanging Pendant Ornaments. NT No. 192 (close-up). *Gyeongju National Museum*

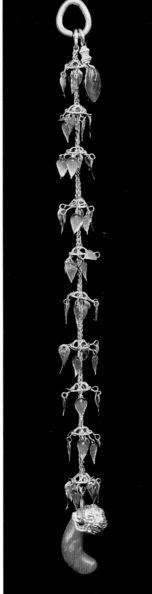

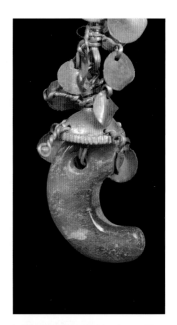

King's Gold Crown. NT No. 87. Fifth century. Multiple three tree-branch and deer-antler design with diadems, comma-shaped jades, and spangles. 10.8". *Gyeongju National Museum*

King's Gold Crown. NT No. 87. Close-up of side long pendant. *Gyeongju National Museum*

King's Gold Crown. NT No. 191. Close-up view of pendants. *Gyeongju National Museum*

King's Gold Crown. NT No. 191. Close-up view of pendants. *Gyeongju National Museum*

Pendants. Wolseong-ro Tomb No. 13. Silla dynasty, end of fourth century. Gold. 4.3". *Gyeongju National Museum*

Gold Pendants. Wolseong-ro Tomb No. 13. Silla dynasty, end of fourth century. Gold. 10.4". *Gyeongju National Museum*

Gold necklace. North mound of Hwangnamdaechong Tomb. Fifth century. 27 cube-shaped open worked rings inside round beads. 10.6". *Gyeongju National Museum*

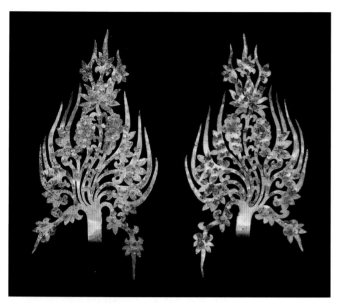

King's Gold Diadem Ornament. NT
No. 154. Sixth century. 127 spangles,
dangling wires with symbols for fire
and flowers. 12.1" × 5.5". *Gongju
National Museum*

Stem Cup with Dangling Ornaments.
North mound of Hwangnamdaechong
Tomb. Silla dynasty, second half of
fifth century. Gold. 3.7". *Gyeongju
National Museum*

Gold Crown. TJ-5061. Excavated
from Gyeongsangnam-do Province,
Three Kingdoms period, 57–676
CE. 6.7". *Tokyo National Museum,
Ogura Collection*

Ax-Cutting Demonstration:
Work Process on *Blue Wings of Kairos Brooch* by PARK Eunju

1. The fish scales are completely dried for at least six months on the netting tray.
2. The scales are dyed with dyestuff.
3. The scales are drilled with two holes, 22 gauge (0.7 mm), then stitched and tied together on one side of the brooch by using translucent fishing line.

박은주 (朴恩珠) PARK Eunju.
Emergence Two. Bracelet. 2013.
3.2" × 3.8" × 2". Sterling-silver
bracelet constructed with hand-cut
and hand-shaped blue-plastic
scales that mimic the appearance
of real fish scales. The scales are
stitched with translucent fishing-
line threads and sewn onto the
pierced silver structure of the
bracelet. These combinations
strengthen the structure and
enhance the airiness of the work.

KIM Jaeyoung's hammer-punch-stitching technique gives surfaces an appearance that resembles fabric quilting. Her vessels are produced with punch-stitching lines as if they are stitched in fabric and quilted on a metal plate.

Kim's work illustrates an ancient Korean cultural tradition that states if a newborn baby wears clothes from one hundred pieces of patched fabrics and one hundred stitched lines of quilted cloth, the baby will live to be one hundred years old.

With this tradition in mind, she hammers and chases lines on the flat silver sheet as if she were embroidering blessings to last one hundred years.

Kim integrates chasing and repoussé (*tachul*) linear lines to create her chasing punches and push out volumes and patterns on the pitch-filled silver vessels. In order to accomplish soft volumes and patterns that resemble a quilted fabric with stitched lines, she incorporates simple punched lines with lightweight hammers.

김재영 (金載瑛) KIM Jaeyoung. *Clean Hand & Pure Heart.* Container. 1984. This vessel has a soft, fabric-like quality as if inviting the viewer to touch. Silver, jade, 24K gold leaf. 7" × 8.7" × 1.8".

김재영 (金載瑛) KIM Jaeyoung. *Tea Kettle & Substantial Pot.* Kettle and pot. 2004. Silver, bamboo. 2.8" × 3.8" × 3.8"; 12.8" × 14" × 4.4".

김재영 (金載瑛) KIM Jaeyoung.
Finding Joy in the Ordinary.
Elongated vessel. 1994. Silver.
3.6" × 14" × 4".

The upper part of the vessel has stitched, quilted lines in a diamond-shaped directional pattern. The enclosed seam is stitched and soldered with three thick, flattened, short wires looking like stitched flattened wires to the main body of the vessel. The elongated oval vessel looks like a traditional basket or aluminum container seen at a farm. The inside of the vessel is gold plated to produce a contrasting effect from the external white frosted colors of the silver vessel.

Medicinal pouch from Saekdong Museum. Twentieth century. The stitching on the quilted fabric was the inspiration for the surface embellishments of Kim Jaeyoung's works.

류연희 (柳延熹) RYU Yeunhee.
Twenty Three Spoons. Silver-spoon
installation. 2015. Created with
traditional Korean techniques of
punched, stitched, and dotted lines
on the very thin silver, but utilizes
contemporary approaches and
setting. Casting, chasing, and
repoussé *(tachu)* surface
techniques. 1.5" × 5" × 1.2" each.

Joinery (*Jangseok*)

Jangseok is traditional decorative joinery used for hinging riveting, and enhancing corners of metal ornaments and practical wooden furniture. *Jangseok* can be seen on chests with stacked drawers, boxes, door frames, handles, and large door locks for gates.

This joinery is created by adding decorative designs with hammer-chisel-chasing or engraving (*jangseok* and *jjoi ipsa*). The decorated metal is then attached to wooden furniture and metal containers such as wedding boxes or locks.

After the Three Kingdoms period (Silla, Goguryeo, and Baekjae dynasties, 57 BCE–676 CE), these techniques can be seen on large door hinges and locks made with iron. In the late Joseon dynasty (1392–1897 CE), bronze locks with simple designs of joinery techniques were popular. Designs with several combinations of metals can be seen on the wooden furniture and large locks for the royal gates and upper-class homes.

The Goryeo dynasty (918–1392 CE) introduced mother-of-pearl overlay to black-lacquered chests, official document boxes, queen's makeup mirrors, and cosmetic boxes. During the Joseon dynasty (1392–1897 CE), many lacquered boxes were used in royal court. The furniture of the upper class featured complicated lacquer containers, detailed with elaborate mother-of-pearl overlay (*najeon chilgi*) and metal joinery decorations. Unlike Chinese and Japanese lacquer works of the time, only Korean works use mother-of-pearl overlay on lacquered (*ottchil*) surfaces for brilliant color and decorative blackened surfaces. Use of *najeon chilgi* technique in royal courts was introduced from the end of the Silla dynasty to the beginning of the Goryeo dynasty (900 CE).

Metals traditionally used for this technique include iron, brass (an alloy of copper and tin), nickel (75% copper, 25% nickel), cupro nickel (an alloy of 75% copper and 25% nickel) and *odong* (an alloy of copper and 6–8% gold, finished with black color). These metals indicate special meanings in designs, such as wealth or class, and they also direct visual focus to meanings or to the center point of the structures.

Traditionally, *odong* was blackened by wrapping a finished work in rice paper, saturating it with stale urine, and then letting it sit in sunlight on a glass sheet for several hours. Contemporary craftspeople substitute ammonia for stale urine to produce a similar effect.

Most decorations were made with white-nickel joinery designs, or even a combination of silver and *odong* designs. These can be seen on large locks or round-shaped designs in the center of special types of chests such as wedding or treasure chests. Metalwork in many different styles was produced for joinery decoration, handles, corner-edge decorations, and the center of the sliding-door handles. Some joinery elements were used on enameled surface decorations of butterfly and bat designs, both of which symbolize good fortune, luck, and happiness.

Traditional designs are usually made with the classical Chinese characters for good luck, happiness, and long life. Other designs depict simplified animal and plant shapes also thought to bring good fortune, blessings, and longevity.

Today, there are many household items made with these traditional *jangseok* decorations. It is not uncommon to see contemporary metalwork that utilizes these traditional techniques.

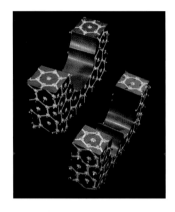

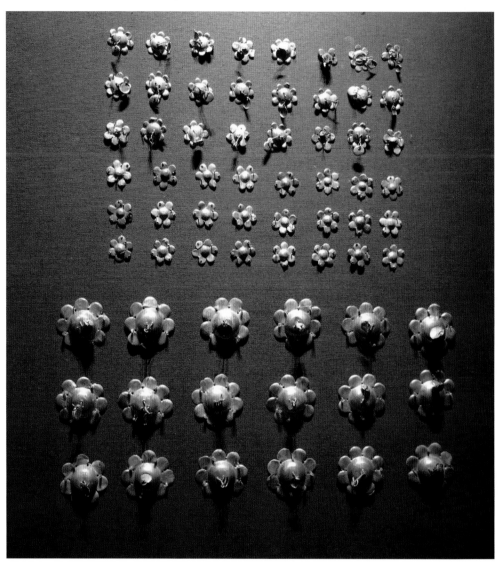

King's Headrest & Footrest. NT No. 165. Sixth century. Wood with *jangseok*, *ottchil* (joinery and Korean sumac lacquer), and gold ornaments. 15". *Gongju National Museum*

Various *jangseok* ornaments. Sixth century. *Gongju National Museum*

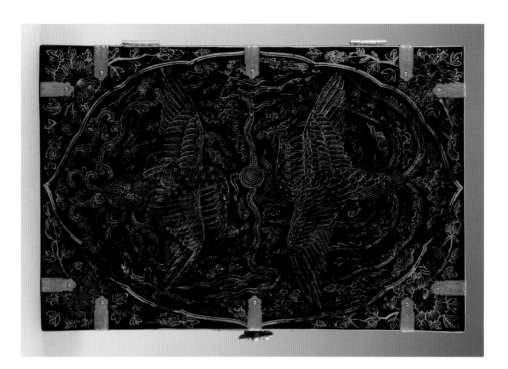

Crown Prince Yeongjo's Official Document Chest, Storing Bamboo Book, Seal, and Other Documents. No. Jongmyo 13490-2. Early nineteenth century, Joseon dynasty. Black lacquer (*ottchil*), wood, 24K gold inscriptions, designs, and patterns. Brass *jangseok*. 10.63" × 16" × 10.55". *National Palace Museum*

Crown Prince Yeongjo's Official Document Chest (Top view). The crown prince's documents were written in a bamboo book (*yoe*-book) with inscripted gold inlaid letters, whereas the king and queen's documents were hammer-chisel-engraved in 24K gold in the jade book, as shown in KIM Young Hee's *Jade Book with Royal Writings* (*page 228*). *National Palace Museum*

3 Drawer Makeup Stand. NT No. 173.
Jangseok ornaments with *ottchil.*
Nickel and wood. 8.4" × 12.4" ×
12.4". *National Palace Museum*

Square Locks with Plum Flower Buds. No. 11-56. Late Joseon dynasty, nineteenth century. Nickel and brass. 0.6" × 2.4" × 2.4" each. Newly budding plum flowers symbolize good news, indicating the end of winter and arrival of spring. Chisel lines and textures of *jangseok. Collection of Lock Museum*

Vermilion-Lacquered Dressing Table Decorated with Brass Plaques Case. No. 91. Joseon dynasty, nineteenth century. Brass, Korean lacquer (*ottchil*), and wood. 13" × 9.8" × 12". *Collection of Koryo Museum, Kyoto, Japan*

Tortoiseshell Seal Case. No. 98. Joseon dynasty, nineteenth century. Brass and wood. 6.6" × 5.2" × 5.2". *Collection of Koryo Museum, Kyoto, Japan*

박문열 PARK Munyeol, National Intangible Cultural Property No. 64: *Duseokjang* Master Craftsperson and Practitioner. *Baeckdong Crayfish Bandaji*. No. 28278. Chest. 2000. Yellow brass and white nickel. *Jangseok*. 25.6" × 16" × 21.2". *National Intangible Cultural Heritage Center*

박문열 PARK Munyeol, National Intangible Cultural Property No. 64: *Duseokjang* Master Craftsperson and Practitioner. *Bandaji with Ten Longevity Symbols*. Chest. No. 28280. 2008. Nickel, copper, brass, wood. *Jangseok*. 43.7" × 19.7" × 18.5". *National Intangible Cultural Heritage Center*

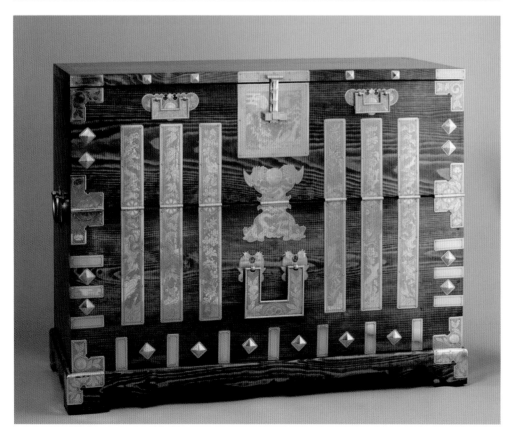

CHO Sung-joon

KOREAN INTANGIBLE PROPERTY NO. 260 MASTER
CRAFTSPERSON & PRACTITIONER

CHO Sung-joon is a master craftsperson who mainly produces replicas of traditional objects, following the historical materials, designs, and techniques. He uses joinery, carving, and hammer-chasing-engraving lines to produce these replicas. All traditional craftspeople create their own alloyed metal sheets, such as white nickel (75% copper, 25% nickel), nickel (70% copper, 18% zinc, 12% nickel), and *odong* (copper with 7%–8% 24K gold). Replica craftspeople such as Cho follow historical techniques, design, and medium precisely for museum replicas. Occasionally, for competitions and personal work, they will use variations of historical designs.

조성준 (趙聖濬) CHO Sung-joon. Korea Intangible Cultural Property No. 260: *Jjoi Ipsa* Master Craftsperson and Practitioner. Candleholding stand on the special enclosed container base. Set of candleholding stands. 1996. Red brass, candle. 6.4" × 6" × 6" each. Used as ornamental candle stands and lighting for royal and upper classes (*yangban*).

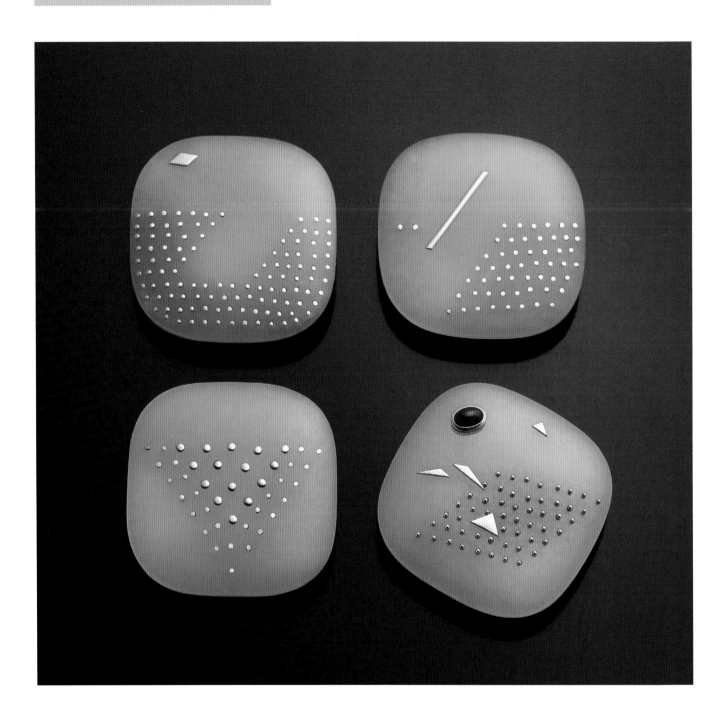

김승희 (金昇姬) KIM Seung Hee.
Four Jade Brooches. Brooches.
1981. White *chuncheon* jade, 14K
gold, coral. Jade carving, drilling,
riveting, and setting. *Jangseok.*
1.9" × 1.9" × 0.2" each.

LEE Jaeik's works are based on traditional joinery (*jangseok*) methods applied to contemporary approaches. His spatial ornamental objects are created through contemporary methods of joinery and riveting.

These rivets are produced through traditional methods but then are welded to hold all cut metal elements. The object is constructed and welded without using the conventional method of raising and constructing to create spatial ornamental vessels.

This process results in the look of traditional techniques—punching and riveting—but is executed in a contemporary manner by welding on a pattern of rivet heads and applying 24K gold leafing (*keumpak*) and fine-silver leafing (*eunbak*) on all rivets and wax-finishing the surface.

이재익 (李在益) LEE Jaeik. *Cavus*. Spatial ornamental vessel. 2014. Copper, 24K gold leaf (*keumpak*). Folding, riveting, welding, and patina. 12.2" × 11" × 11".

Cavus was formed with a traditional technique of riveting (*jangseok*), but by way of welding dots and applying 24K gold with gold leaf to create a strong, contrasting effect.

이재익 (李在益) LEE Jaeik. *Verietas*. Spatial ornamental vessel. 2016. Copper, 24K gold leaf (*keumpak*), patina. Folding, stitching, riveting, welding, and patina. 18.3" × 11.6" × 11.6".

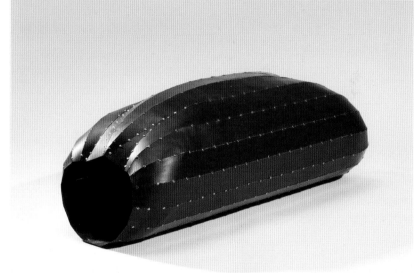

CHAPTER 2

Inlay Techniques

Line Inlay: *Seon Ssanggum (Kkium Ipsa)*

Line inlay (*kkium ipsa*) is the inlaying of thin (0.25–0.3 mm) pure metal threads into base metals such as iron and bronze. *Kkium ipsa* uses a chiseling tool and hammer to first cut a groove into the face of metal and then cut in two more different directional cuts to the same line. This will make a groove to create protruding edges, which will allow the inlaid pure metal wires such as fine gold, silver, and copper to be held in.

This inlay technique was introduced from the Han dynasty of China during the Korean Three Kingdoms period. Gold, silver, and copper threads filled patterns detailed into vessels, boxes, and incense burners. This technique became very popular, producing many ceremonial objects in royal court. Korea's own style of inlay became prominent during the late Goryeo dynasty (918–1392 CE). Buddhist items and royal court containers demonstrate the use of this technique, such as incense burners, sword handles and cases, ewers for ceremonial proceedings, and makeup cases.

During the Three Kingdoms period (57 BCE–676 CE), *kkium ipsa* (line inlay technique) was very popular for decorating Buddhist religious items, royal ceremonial objects, incense burners, and containers. Several well-known artifacts from the Three Kingdoms period, such as a copper and iron footrest, can be seen in the collection of the National Museum of Korea. These objects were made mostly with fine-silver and gold wire inlay on copper containers, but incense-burner artifacts were made with iron and inlaid with fine-silver and copper threads.

This technique involves inserting nonferrous metal threads into the finished object, made from a base metal (iron, copper, or bronze). Thin, narrow chisel-like chasing tools are used to cut continuous lines into the base metal. A ditch is hollowed, with walls slanting into an angular U shape *(see drawing)*. The angles allow the edges to retain the fine wires that will be inlaid inside the ditches. The fine-silver, gold, or copper wires (0.25–0.3 mm) are inserted to form the desired patterns. Most designs are created by repeated wire inlay of the desired width and shapes. The shapes are created with thin foil patterns introduced with a Korean chiseled ditch, hammered in with the same size of very thin foil inlaid to the shape to emphasize lines and shapes.

Historically, the most-common designs were patterns of clouds, deer, willow trees, dragons, and peacocks. In later periods, personal ornamental containers, mirrors, and eating utensils were decorated with poetical landscapes like drawings, with mythical symbols and with Chinese characters of good fortune. Many of the designs expressed wishes for longevity, fertility, male offspring, happiness, and prosperity.

These metal items were so important that the Silla dynasty had an inlaying craft center dedicated solely to producing these ceremonial objects for the royal court.

Nowadays, craftspeople who are dedicated to creating historical replicas make traditional objects for wedding ceremonies and Buddhist temples, with clients ordering through commercial crafts shops dealing in silver and gold as well as government-designated craftspeople with titles (important Intangible Cultural Properties master practitioners).

Today, many artists use this technique for ornaments and jewelry that combine traditional methods with contemporary designs.

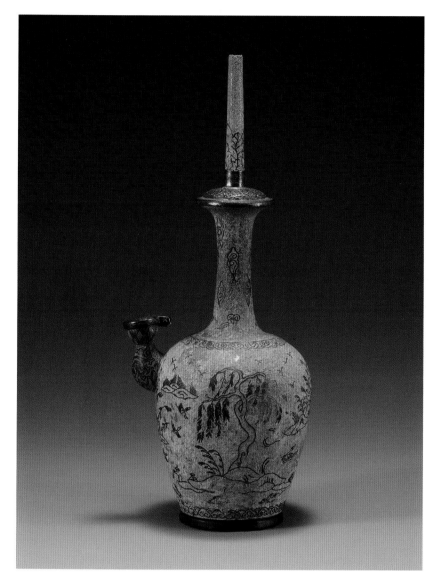

Ritual Ewer (Kundika). NT No. 92.
Goryeo dynasty, twelfth century.
Silver (inlaid) *kkium ipsa* on bronze.
14.9". *National Museum of Korea*

Small Brazier (Burner). Duk2606.
Joseon dynasty, nineteenth
century. Copper. *Kkium ipsa* (silver
seon-ssanggum inlay) and *jjoeum
ipsa* with 12 Longevity beings.
8.4". *National Museum of Korea*

*Cigarette Box with Plum and
Bamboo Design*. Nam02508.
Joseon dynasty, nineteenth
century. *Jjoeum ipsa* and *jjoigil*
(silver and gold line inlay
ssanggum) on copper. 3.1".
National Museum of Korea

Bronze Jar. Unified Silla dynasty,
ninth–tenth centuries. *Kkium ipsa*
(gold and silver *seon-ssanggum* inlay).
3.1". *National Museum of Korea*

Youi. S-shaped ceremonial
ornament. Joseon dynasty,
nineteenth century. *Kkium ipsa*
(silver *ssanggum* inlay) on brass.
19.5". *National Museum of Korea*

Line Inlay (*Kkium Ipsa*) Leaf Vessel Demonstration by KIM Yong-Woon

NATIONAL INTANGIBLE CULTURAL PROPERTY NO. 35: *JOGAK* MASTER AND PRACTITIONER

(NOTE: A *JOGAK* IS AN ADVANCED METALSMITH WHO CAN EXECUTE ALL TRADITIONAL METAL FORMING AND INLAYING TECHNIQUES)

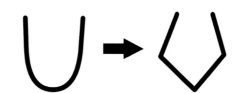

Side cut view, cross section of *kkium ipsa* (*seon ssanggum*).

Kkium ipsa is a method of inserting another thread into a base metal by chisel-hammer-engraving into the base metal of the work. Hammering on the pointed chasing-engraving tool cuts grooves for the inlay.

1. There are two different methods for inlaying (inserting) different-colored metal threads such as fine-silver or fine-gold threadlike wires into a base metal (object or vessel). One is by chisel-hammer-engraving-cutting into the base object with a very sharp cutting chisel (chasing tool with sharp tip, 0.08–0.12 cm wide). The second method involves using a sharp-pointed chisel tool 0.04 cm wide (*tchoii-jung*) to create inlaying, called dot inlay (*jeom ipsa*). One must consider the hardness and thickness of the base metal object for inlaying, and hammer with the appropriate hammer-cutting-engraving to the base metal object. The length of this cutting chisel is about 3.4 cm.
2. The length of the hammer is 8.5 cm, plus or minus. The hammerhead length is 24 cm, and the head is 3 cm with a diameter of 1.8 cm.
3. Draw a pattern on the base metal (object) with a scribe (or a magic marker) and cut in grooves with the cutting chisel tool.
4. When making the first groove, cut straight down by slanting the tool into a slight angle for cutting grooves. Make sure the grooves are not too deep or shallow.
5. The grooves are cut in various thicknesses to make the pattern stand out. Be careful not to inlay too deeply.

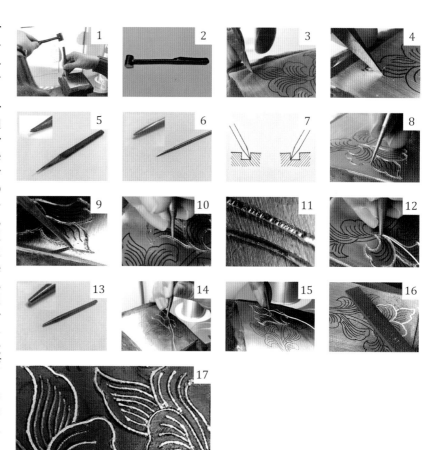

Broader lines: Approximately: 0.6–0.7 mm width × 0.6 mm depth

Normal lines: Approximately: 0.38–0.42 mm width × 0.4 mm depth

Thin lines: Approximately: 0.2–0.25 mm width × 0.3 mm depth

6. One must be careful not to break the tip of the cutting tool when cutting around curves.
7. Pointed cutting tool for cutting in inside of the line (design): 7 cm long × 3 mm diameter
8. Hammer the sharp-pointed tool into the center of the groove, then to the left and right to hollow the ditch.
9. Ditch out the grooves and inside corner lines, cut out as closely (densely) as cut corners with a sharp-pointed tool.
10. Hammer hard until hammer marks are seen closely in the opposing side of the groove.
11. Work on the opposite edge of the design, same manner as above.

12. The line at the top of the picture shows properly dug-out grooves. The bottom line shows the cut groove before it is hammered.
13. After using no. 16 tool, inlay silver wire. The groove and the silver wire width should be same thickness.
14. An inserting tool: tool for inlaying silver thread into the groove. The appropriate thickness depends on the thickness of the thread being inlaid. The thickness of the thread should match the groove.
15. When inlaying the silver wire, hammer hard to make sure the wire gets into the grooves.
16. If silver thread is hammered too hard or too many times, the wire will stretch and not be properly inlaid.
17. When the inlaying process is finished, the surface is ground with a file and finished with fine sandpaper. After a final coloring (see Black C Coloring instructions), the vessel is coated with beeswax to complete the project.

Black C Coloring Instructions: Coloring after *Kkium Ipsa* (*Seon Ssanggum*) by KIM Yong-Woon

NATIONAL INTANGIBLE CULTURAL PROPERTY NO. 35: *JOGAK* MASTER AND PRACTITIONER

Black C Solution: ratio of 5:1 of sodium chlorate and caustic soda (solution coloring is blue)
1. Clean the object in the hot pickle bath to take off all greased surface, and rinse under running faucet water.
2. Repeat cleaning process in the hot pickle bath until surface is well cleaned (cleaning may be repeated till the object is oil free).
3. Keep the object in 104°F (40°C) hot water and immerse the object in the Black C Patina Solution.
4. Leave the object till the blackness color is achieved. Rinse the object under running water and pat dry the copper vessel with very clean soft rag.
5. Rub with wax and buff for the final coating.

김용운 (金龍雲) KIM Yong-Woon, National Intangible Cultural Property No. 35: *Jogak* Master and Practitioner. *Bronze Vase 1*. Vase. 2008. Raising, forming, and line inlay (*kkium ipsa*). Bronze, fine-silver wire inlay, patina. 5.9" × 9.1" × 9.1" (demonstration piece).

Jogak means metal surface sculpting using hammer-smithing/raising and the *seon ssanggum* (*kkium ipsa*) techniques. The practitioner is called *jogakjang*. He is a master of creating vessels as well as the surface *kkium ipsa* embellishing techniques.

KIM Yong-Woon

Small CAPS: NATIONAL INTANGIBLE CULTURAL PROPERTY NO.
35: *JOGAK* MASTER AND PRACTITIONER

Traditional craftspeople such as Kim Yong-Woon use their own alloyed metal sheets (98% pure silver, 1% alloy) for silver and gold teapots. For silver teapots, a 22K gold wire is used (91.7% gold, 6.5% silver, 1.8% copper). For bronze or copper vessels or objects, silver wire is used (99% silver, 1% alloy).

김용운 (金龍雲) KIM Yong-Woon, National Intangible Cultural Property No. 35: *Jogak* Master and Practitioner. *Bronze Phoenix Ewer & Basin.* Ceremonial ewer and basin. 2017. Drawing quality of historical shapes of phoenix and dragon with arabesque, peony, water lily, and water landscape patterns is emphasized. Raising, forming, fabricating, chasing and repoussé (*tachul*), and line inlay (*kkium ipsa*). Bronze container, platinum and 24K gold wire inlay, patina, wax coating. 13.2" × 9.8" × 6.4"; 6.6" × 8" × 8". *Artist replicated shape from the Museum of Fine Arts, Boston but added own inlay patterns and phoenix handle*

김용운 (金龍雲) KIM Yong-Woon, National Intangible Cultural Property No. 35: *Jogak* Master and Practitioner. Ceremonial powder tea container. 2014. Forming, constructing, and inlaid with *kkium ipsa*. Silver, 24K gold wire inlay. 3" × 3.4" × 3.4".

김용운 (金龍雲) KIM Yong-Woon, National Intangible Cultural Property No. 35: *Jogak* Master and Practitioner. *Tea Container with Silver Box Inside with Jade-Wonang Bird Knob and Stand.* Container. 2017. The outer bronze container has a silver tea container inside. The silver container has the knob, jade duck (*Wonang* bird; a symbol of lasting love). Bronze, 24K gold wire, silver, patina, carved jade. 2.32" × 2.16" × 2.16".

김용운 (金龍雲) KIM Yong-Woon,
National Intangible Cultural Property
No. 35: *Jogak* Master and
Practitioner. *Bronze Vase with
Leaves*. No. FE.86-2017. Flower
vase. 2008. Raising, forming, filing
finish, *kkium ipsa* (line inlaying)
finishing in the pitch. Bronze,
fine-silver wire, black patina on
copper, and wax coating finish. 7.6"
× 7.2" × 7.2". *Collection of Victoria
and Albert Museum, London*

DESIGNATED EDUCATIONAL ASSISTANT
INSTRUCTOR FOR TRAINING NO. 35: *JOGAKJANG*
(METAL ENGRAVING)

NAM Kyung Sook's works are created with the traditional techniques of line inlay (*kkium ipsa*) and Korean-style damascene (*jjoeum ipsa*) techniques on iron and copper backgrounds, with inlay of fine-silver wires.

These objects, holloware, and jewelry are constructed with sterling silver, copper, and brass. The ritual objects and ornaments with various contemporary designs are based on traditional motifs.

남경숙 (南庚淑) NAM Kyung Sook.
Designated assistant instructor for training for *jogakjang* (metal sculpting-hammer-chisel-engraving and *seon ssanggum*). *Song of Flowers*. Container. 2015. *Kkium ipsa* and *jjoeum ipsa*. Iron, copper, fine-silver wire, 24K and 18K gold, iron, patina. 5.6" × 9.2" × 9.2".

남경숙 (南庚淑) NAM Kyung
Sook. Designated assistant
instructor for training for *jogakjang*
(metal sculpting-hammer-chisel-
engraving and *seon ssanggum*).
Beyond the Clouds. Container.
2014. *Kkium ipsa.* Copper,
fine-silver wire, brass, patina. 6.4"
× 9.2" × 9.2".

KIM Jong-kuk and KIM Jong-bong

GOVERNMENT-DESIGNATED EDUCATION
ASSISTANTS TO MASTER KIM YONG-WOON.

These two assistants use the traditional methods of making their own alloyed wires in their inlays and sheet metals.

For silver teapots, a 22K gold wire is used (91.7% gold, 6.5% silver, 1.8% copper). For bronze or copper vessels or objects, silver wire is used (99% silver, 1% alloy).

김종국 (金鐘國) KIM Jong-kuk. *Flower Vase on Stand*. Silver flower vase on bronze base. 2017. *Kkium ipsa*. Platinum, 24K yellow gold wire and fine silver wire, patina. 4.8" × 4.8" × 4.8".

김종봉 (金鐘鳳) KIM Jong-bong.
Education assistant to Master KIM
Yong-Woon. *Incense Burner with
Phoenix Handle on Bronze Base.*
Vessel on bronze base. 2017.
Kkium ipsa. Bronze vessel with
alloyed platinum and 24K yellow
gold wires, patina. 6" × 6" × 6".

주예경 (周禮敬) CHOO Yae Kyung. *The Sky above Seoul.* Object. 1987. Forming, constructing, fabricating, and line-inlaying (*kkium ipsa*) techniques. Steel, fine silver. 2.5" × 18" × 10".

These are contemporary objects with functional purposes. The designs are simple and clean but were made through sophisticated traditional techniques.

주예경 (周禮敬) CHOO Yae Kyung. *The Flower Vase.* Vase. 1987. Raising, forming, planishing, fabricating, and line inlay (*kkium ipsa*) and patina. Copper, 24K gold, fine silver. 37.5" × 15" × 15".

SHIN Jae Hyup uses traditional Korean line inlay technique on the lip areas of his vessels. Vessel 2-IV-P-1 was hammered on rocks instead of employing regular metalsmith techniques.

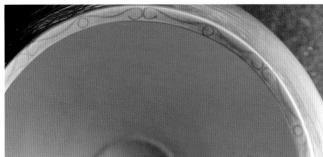

신재협 (申載硤) SHIN Jae Hyup. *Vessel 2-IV-P-1*. Vessel. 2004. Raising, constructing, texturing outside bowl on the stone. Copper bowl with fine-silver wire inlay on the top of the lid and framed like stone-setting/marriage metals (*jeoul ipsa*), line inlay (*kkium ipsa*) on the lip of the vessel, and chemical patina on outside of vessel. 9" × 21" × 21".

신재협 (申載硤) SHIN Jae Hyup. *Vessel 4*. Vessel. 2011. *Kkium ipsa*. Sterling-silver vessel with 24K gold wire inlay on the lip of the bowl. Outside bowl is textured and inside of the bowl is gold plated to coincide with the gold wire inlay on the lip of the bowl. 7" × 6" × 6".

신재협 (申載硤) SHIN Jae Hyup. *Vessel 4* (top view).

조성혜 (趙星慧) CHO Sung Hae. *Day of Tales*. Vessel. 2007. Raised, formed, constructed, enameled (*chilbo*), line inlaid (*kkium ipsa*) patina, and 24K gold leaf (*keumpak*) over enameled vessel. 24K gold leaf, fine silver, copper, iron. 7.2" × 6" × 6".

Traditional techniques are applied with detailed contemporary designs of contrasting black, white, and gold colors. These table pieces are designed to be simple and functional.

조성혜 (趙星慧) CHO Sung Hae. *The Leaves*. Paperweights. 2002. Formed, constructed, detailed with line inlay (*kkium ipsa*) designs with fine-silver and copper wires on iron block. Iron, fine silver, copper, patina. 1.8" × 2.4" × 2.4" each.

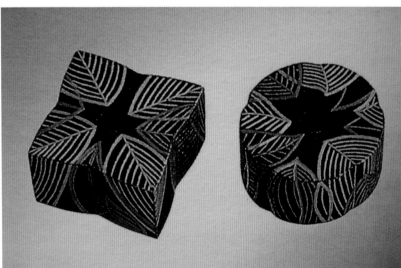

Korean Damascene: *Poamock Ssanggum*
(Jjoeum Ipsa)

Korean damascene (*jjoeum ipsa*), previously called *poamock ssanggum*, looks like inlay in woven cloth.

This traditional technique was introduced into Korea from Spain through the Silk Road. It developed starting in the fourth century and would flourish during the Joseon dynasty (1832–1897 CE). It was used on iron surfaces and royal palace items such as incense burners, swords, mirror stands, candleholders, cigarette boxes, pencil and brush containers, large iron locks, portable iron charcoal burners, cosmetic items, and decorative objects.

The technique was called *poamock ssanggum* ("cloths inlay") during the Japanese occupation of Korea and was recently designated by historians as *jjoeum ipsa* (inlay on chiseled surface). The former name described the appearance. The latter name describes the method of chiseling four directional cuts with a knife-edge-sharp chasing tool. The method creates a cloth-like chiseled surface that accepts the fine, thin wire (well-annealed fine metals of 0.02–0.03 mm thin wire and foil).

The inlay is established by using a chiseling motion, which raises burrs on the iron, preparing the surface for metal inlay. In this method, unlike *kkium ipsa*, high-speed steel chisels are struck straight down into the base material with a metal hammer. A pattern of closely spaced parallel grooves running crisscross from four different directions is established in order to accept the metal inlay. Fine metal threads and sheet metal (0.025–0.03 mm) are then laid on the prepared surface in a manner that mimics a fine pencil drawing.

The most-frequent designs used from the Three Kingdoms period to the Silla dynasty (fourth to ninth centuries) were the symbolic patterns for longevity: clouds, deer, willow trees, dragons, and peacocks. In the later periods, commoners adopted these methods for domestic craft objects, including wearable ornaments, mirrors, eating utensils (decorating the handles), candleholders, pencil holders, cigarette boxes, and large furniture/door hinges and locks. Many of these objects were decorated with lyrical waterside landscapes, mystical symbols of authority such as dragons and phoenixes, and Sanskrit characters, as well as various arabesque patterns. Designs often express the blessings and eternal-youth emblems of bats, carp designs, flowers, and blooming foliage.

Club. Joseon dynasty, 1392–1897 CE. Silver inlay (*ssanggum*) on iron. 20.5". *National Museum of Korea*

Club (close-up). *National Museum of Korea*

Club (close-up). *National Museum of Korea*

Hinge and Handle Ornaments. Joseon dynasty, 1392–1897 CE. Silver inlay (*jjoeum ipsa*) on iron. 4.1". *National Museum of Korea*

Craftsperson
Technical References

Traditional Method of Korean Damascene (*Jjoeum Ipsa*) Demonstration

Produced by HONG Jungsil, the National Intangible Cultural Property No. 78: Inlay (*ipsa*) Master and the director of the Gilkeum Research Institute. Demonstrated by KIM Sunjung, research assistant to Gilkeum Metal Crafts Research Institute.

1. The iron vessel is filled with *gamtang*, a melted mixture of resin and earth powder similar to pitch.
2. The surface is evenly chiseled with rows as closely as 1 mm from one another with a sharp-edged-tip chasing tool, the *jung*.
3. Chisel repeatedly in four different directions, at an angle of 45 degrees from one another. This demonstration shows chiseling from the right side to the left side (but one can chisel from bottom to top).
4. The design is traced on very thin tracing paper, which is placed over carbon paper on the surface of the vessel. The design is then outlined over the entire surface by tapping dotted lines with a sharp tipped tool over the traced pattern.
5. This metal thread is applied by hammering into the chiseled surface to highlight the shapes and pattern of the design.
6. The inlaid design areas are secured by hammering over with *saseum-ppul*, a rod made from deer horn.
7. The object is emptied of pitch and cleaned in *yangjaet mool*, which is a caustic soda solution.
8. The surface is coated with *gumdaeng*, a mixture of soot and vegetable oil, and heated to get a black-colored surface.
9. The design is scraped with *galgi*, a sharp-edged scraper, to expose the inlaid design. The surface is filed and smoothed with sandpaper.
10. The surface is finished with warm vegetable oil for permanence.

NATIONAL INTANGIBLE CULTURAL PROPERTY NO.
78: INLAY (*IPSA*) MASTER AND PRACTITIONER IN
JJOEUM IPSA

Hong's work is characterized by Korean
damascene inlay (*jjoeum ipsa*) on iron, created by hammer-chiseling, with four directional cuts having as little as 0.5 mm space
between each line. Korean traditional motifs
in contemporary settings inspire Hong's
creative work. She bases her chosen themes
and motifs on traditional scenes, patterns,
and background images, and she expresses
them through her personal aesthetic.

홍정실 (洪正實) HONG Jungsil.
National Intangible Cultural
Property No. 78: Inlay (*Jjoeum Ipsa*)
Master and Practitioner. *Deep
Spring Sub-consciousness.* Vessel.
2003. *Jjoeum ipsa* and *ottchil.*
   24K gold, 18K gold, fine silver,
iron, brass, lacquers. 9" × 12" ×
12". This piece expands depth and
distance into three-dimensional
space by attaching and inserting
metal pieces sparsely on the
work's body.
   Process for *Deep Spring
Sub-consciousness*:
   1. The body is formed.
   2. The surface is inlaid with
      silver threads.
   3. The metal parts are attached
      to the body.
   4. The body is painted with
      Korean lacquer.
   5. The painted lacquer is
      scraped to reveal the inlaid
      parts on the body.

홍정실 (洪正實) HONG Jungsil. National Intangible Cultural Property No. 78: Inlay (*Jjoeum Ipsa*) Master and Practitioner. *Feast of Wild Flowers*. Vessel. 1989. *Jjoeum ipsa*. Application of Korean sumac lacquering (*ottchil*), after an inlay with fine-silver and fine-gold threads (*jjoeum ipsa* and *ottchil*). 24K gold, 18K gold, fine silver, iron, copper, lacquer. 6" × 18.5" × 18.5". This work expresses the joy and life of wild, grassy fields. It reflects the artist's affection for the small things in nature that are barely noticeable, such as field flowers, bees and insects, or the sounds of insects, whispering winds, and the rustle of fallen leaves.

This work was Hong's first creative production using the application of Korean sumac lacquering (*ottchil*), after an inlay with fine-silver and fine-gold threads (*jjoeum ipsa* and *ottchil*). After completing the work with *jjoeum ipsa*, Hong applied *ottchil* processes twice with black *ottchil*, then baked the work in a kiln. The resulting final black-lacquered surface was scraped to reveal the inlaid areas.

홍정실 (洪正實) HONG Jungsil. National Intangible Cultural Property No. 78: Inlay (*Jjoeum Ipsa*) Master and Practitioner. *The Light*. Container. 2014. *Jjoeum ipsa* and *ottchil*. In this piece, overlapped silver threads blend together as if shining through an open doorway, representing beams of light. The colors harmonize, with the surface's textures extended far beyond the colors. 24K gold, 18K gold, fine silver, copper, iron, lacquer. 5.7" × 13.6" × 6.6".

Process for *The Light*:
1. The iron body was formed.
2. After being inlaid with silver threads, the surface was painted with Korean lacquer (*ottchil*). The surface was painted and heated repeatedly seven times with different-colored lacquers.
3. The painted lacquer surface was scraped to reveal silver thread inlay (*jjoeum ipsa*) designs and coated with clear lacquer.

AHN Yong Hee

IMPORTANT TRADITIONAL HANDICRAFT HOLDERS,
78TH INLAYER COMPLETION

AHN Yong Hee wants to carry on traditional techniques while combining them with contemporary styles and designs in conjunction with today's lifestyle and culture. She combines traditional technique and colorful patterns with the contemporary simplicity of black, adding 24K gold *keumpak* (gold leaf) to accentuate the drama.

안용희 (安龍姬) AHN Yong Hee. Important Traditional Handicraft Holders No. 78: Inlayer Completion. *Human Plus Human.* Container. 2006. She emphasizes the traditional *jjoeum ipsa* technique in the contemporary settings, patterns, and functions. Iron container with fine-silver wire inlay. 8" × 5" × 5".

안용희 (安龍姬) AHN Yong Hee. Important Traditional Handicraft Holders No. 78: Inlayer Completion. *Lotus Flower.* Container. 2007. Traditional *jjoeum ipsa* and *keumpak* techniques in the contemporary settings, patterns, and aesthetics are expressed in this work. Iron vessel with fine-silver wire inlay and 24K gold *keum-boo* overlay and *keumpak* (24K gold leaf). 5" × 4" × 4" (top view).

HWANG BO Ji Young

IMPORTANT TRADITIONAL HANDICRAFT HOLDERS,
78TH INLAYER COMPLETION

HWANG BO Ji Young uses traditional techniques in contemporary designs to create
functional objects. After *jjoeum ipsa* is
completed, the containers are coated with
sumac lacquering to preserve the inlay work.

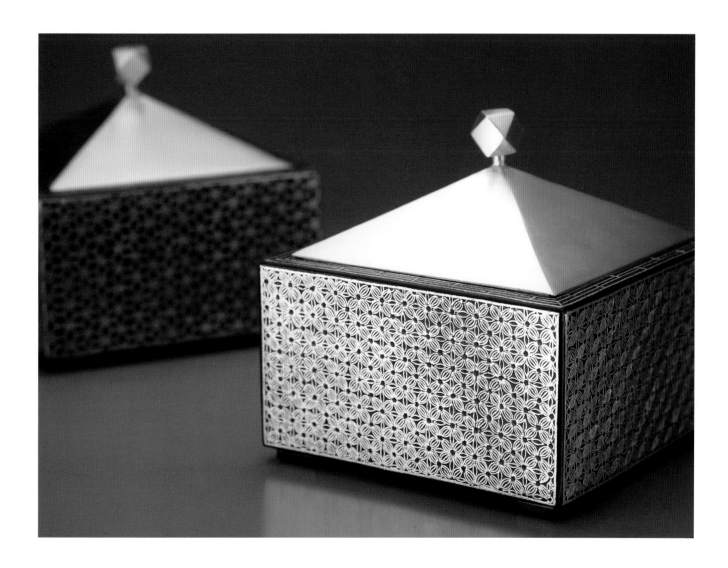

황보지영 (皇甫知暎) HWANG BO
Ji Young. Important Traditional
Handicraft Holders No. 78: Inlayer
Completion. *Time*. Wedding chests.
2010. *Jjoeum ipsa* and *ottchil*. Iron,
fine and sterling silver, Korean
lacquer (*ottchil*). 6" × 5" × 5" each.

KIM Sunjung

ASSISTANT AND RESEARCHER TO *GILKEUM* METAL
CRAFTS RESEARCH INSTITUTE

김선정 (金宣廷) KIM Sunjung. *Great Joy*. Brooch. 2007. Korean damascene (*jjoeum ipsa*), Korean sumac lacquering (*ottchil*). 24K gold, 18K gold, 14K gold wire, sheet inlay on iron sheet, setting with South Sea *keshi* pearl, diamond, citrine, Korean sumac lacquer patina finish. 2.4" × 4.3" × 0.7".

The structure of nature is wonderful in itself. How great is the principle of creation in a small flower! By cutting, bending, and joining with thin, fine-line inlays on iron plates, I am just playing with the flower while creating images with inlay lines.

김선정 (金宣廷) KIM Sunjung. *The Birth*. Brooch. 2007. Korean damascene (*jjoeum ipsa*), Korean sumac lacquering (*ottchil*). 24K gold, 18K gold, 14K gold wires and foil inlay on iron plate set with South Sea *keshi* pearl, diamond setting, and Korean sumac lacquer patina finish. 3.3" × 2.2" × 1".

The whimsical form created by nature was the germ of the idea. A pearl became a sitting bird, and the overlapping multiple petals became a nest. As the bird sits, a history of life begins in the nest. The gold lines are inlaid on the iron background and announce the expansion of life.

KIM Moonjung

ASSISTANT AND RESEARCHER TO GILKEUM METAL
CRAFTS RESEARCH INSTITUTE

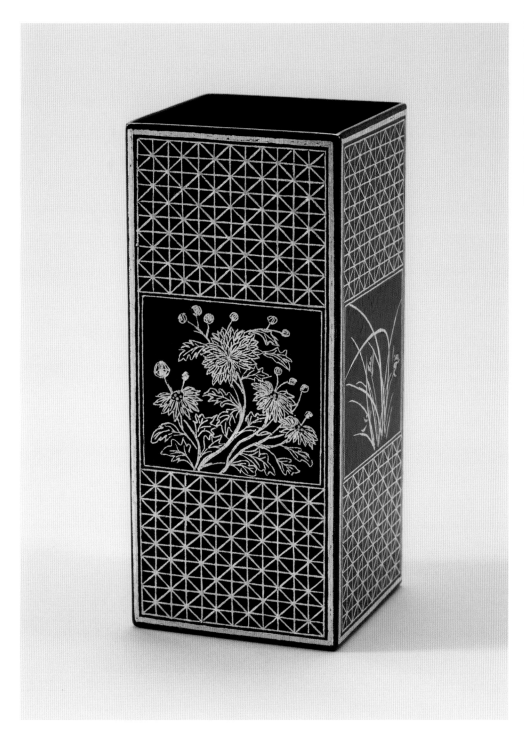

김문정 (金紋廷) KIM Moonjung. *Iron Brush Holder with 4 Graceful Plants.* Container. 2016. 24K gold and fine-silver wire inlay on iron with sumac lacquer technique. 6.7" × 3" × 3".

This a brush stand with the four Graceful Plants (plum, orchid, chrysanthemum, and bamboo) decorated with Korean-style damascene inlay (*jjoeum ipsa*). These graceful plants symbolize a gentleman with high character in the Confucian culture of Korea.

Contemporary Preparation for Setting Mild-Steel-Damascened Flat Piecework to Jewelry or Objects by Komelia Hongja Okim

1. Prepare flat sheet of 18- or 16-gauge mild steel (iron is used traditionally). This sheet is evenly chiseled, with each cut placed as close as 0.3–0.5 mm from the next. The chiseling process creates a Velcro-like barbed surface that can lock in applied surface design elements consisting of fine-silver, 24K gold, and/or copper foil or fine-gauge annealed wires.

2. The metal sheet is placed on pitch, an anvil, or a thick steel block and secured with double-faced tape.

3. A sharp, straight-edged chisel with a V-shaped tip is used to incise a crosshatched pattern (at least 1 mm deep) by chisel-cutting with repeated chopping motions swept across the plate from four directions at 45-degree angles from one another:

   (a) Hold the chisel between the thumb and index finger of the left hand about 1" (2.54 cm) above the cutting edge and move the side of your wrists with the pinky finger, ring, and middle fingers, sweeping upward (or right to left) as you strike the chisel head with a chasing hammer with your right hand. Your elbow should be held slightly raised and horizontally, and the head of the chisel should be kept pointing toward you at an angle of approximately 10 degrees.

   (b) Begin cutting the first vertical or horizontal row by chiseling in columns, placing each column touching and adjacent to the next. Continue until the entire surface is chiseled. You may start chiseling row by row either from the right side to the left of the plate, or from the bottom to the top.

   (c) Rotate the plate 90 degrees and repeat the chiseling cuts.

   (d) Rotate the plate 90 degrees and chisel the third set of diagonal cuts.

   (e) Rotate the plate 90 degrees and chisel the fourth set of diagonal cuts.

4. Create and establish the inlay design:

   (a) Since fine-gold, silver, and copper foils (foil, not leaf: 0.3 mm or 38 to 42 gauge) are extremely delicate, you must place the foils between two sheets of tracing paper before cutting the design with an X-Acto knife (or sharp, fine surgical scissors). Place the cut-foil shapes according to your design and tap lightly in place with a narrow-faced riveting hammer (0.5" or 1 cm or less faced riveting hammer).

   (b) Draw the desired lines or patterns with a scribe on the chisel-cut plate.

   (c) Place the end of the wire (0.25–0.3 mm) at the beginning of your line and lightly tap into place, using a 0.5" faced riveting hammer to tap along the line as if you are drawing with the wire.

   (d) Once all inlays are initially established, the inlaid design areas can be covered with cellophane or a layer of a thin plastic bag, then locked in more securely by gently using a small, lightweight riveting hammer.

   (e) When the inlaid design is complete, transparent tape is laid lightly over the *jjoeum ipsa* design to protect it while refining the final shape of the edge of the steel plate. The edge contour of the shape is sawed, filed, and sanded in a "downward" direction with files and emery paper. The tape will keep the filings and dust from going into the chiseled base.

   (f) The tape must be removed gently in case any part of the inlaid elements is not fully secure. If any inlaid element is not fully secure or dislodging occurs, additional hammering is repeated at that site with the chasing hammer.

5. The gray color of the mild steel can be darkened to a black tone through a heat patina.

   (a) Place the inlaid steel plate on an elevated wire rack on a tripod; "face up" with the inlay on top.

   (b) Heat only the underside of the mild-steel plate with an annealing flame, while observing the color change of the steel from the top surface. Do not allow the flame to touch the top inlay, and continue slow heating from underneath until the desired black of the mild steel is achieved, offering greater contrast to the gold and silver inlay.

   (c) Drop the hot piece into a deep can of clean motor oil and immediately cover with a lid or a thick piece of cardboard. This is necessary to avoid breathing fumes. Remove the cooled piece after a few minutes and dab off the motor oil by pressing between clean soft cloths until no more oil comes off.

   (d) Once cooled, the *jjoeum ipsa* design is sprayed lightly with a clear Krylon metal fixative, or a polyurethane sealant spray, with two to three light coats to seal the surface on front and back. Each coat should have a drying time of 20 minutes before the next coat is applied.

6. The completed *jjoeum ipsa* inlay is then set into place in the jewelry or holloware design, along with any other stone settings and cold connections that remain.

OKIM Komelia Hongja

김홍자 (金弘子) OKIM Komelia Hongja. *One Fine Day*. Nine-section dry-food container. 2016. *Jjoeum ipsa* and *ottchil*, raising, forming, texturing, casting lily flower buds as prongs, Korean damascene on mild steel, setting, constructing, oxidizing, sumac *ottchil* coating finish. Fine and sterling silver, mild steel. 8" × 27" × 25".

This water-lily-pond container combines contemporary techniques and design with Korean traditional techniques and themes. To keep the dry food contained inside fresh, the container is coated with a *keumtaechil-ottchil* coating.

Komelia Okim came to Southern Illinois University, Edwardsville, as an inspiring guest artist, where through many workshops she brought *keum-boo* and *poamock saang-gum* to Myers's students and other faculty. Every workshop included the history of Korean metalsmithing techniques as well as Korean culture. The dynamic surface embellishment resulting from these techniques demonstrated by Okim's presentations and her work enriched and inspired students in their own future personal and aesthetic application.

김홍자 (金弘子) OKIM Komelia Hongja. *Sunday Outing, Fine Day.* Brooch. 1990. *Jjoeum ipsa* and *keum-boo* overlay techniques. Fine and sterling silver, mild steel, fine-silver wire inlay. *Private collection, Washington DC*
The French painter George Seurat's *Sunday Afternoon at the Park* influenced this brooch with architectural design concept, adding contemporary setting and techniques. All units are mitered and applied in 3-D setting as a wearable small sculpture. Black oxidation around *keum-boo* on 24K gold overlay application shows a strong window view of the inside and outside of the landscape.

김홍자 (金弘子) OKIM Komelia Hongja. *Moonscape I & II.* Brooches. 1986. Sterling silver, 24K gold foil, fine-silver foil, mild steel, oxidation. *Collection of Racine Museum of Fine Arts & Linda Threadgill*
Moonscape views with Korean damascene (*jjoeum ipsa*) and *keum-boo* overlay techniques are applied inside the round, window-view-setting brooches. The concept of window view landscape is represented with abstract designs of simple geometric shapes in front of black, round moon shapes.

CHO Namu expresses his aesthetic values through talisman objects highlighting special events. His patterns and motifs are based on his personal vision combined with Korean traditions and symbolic meanings. These pieces are reflections on his heritage, personal aspirations, and imagination.

Cho works with the technique of Korean style of damascene (*jjoeum ipsa*). Cho's damascene technique resembles riveted domed dots instead of dot inlay (*jeom ssanggam*), with identical cutout round shapes of gold sheet. The dot-like round-dome inlays add a strong quality, looking like granules. These round, repeated, inlaid dome circles contrast with the black-steel background, with many small diamond settings looking like a starry night. Cho's art jewelries are executed with Korean traditional style of damascene techniques but are approached, executed, and utilized uniquely in his own style.

조남우 (趙南宇) CHO Namu. *Sprite 1.* Brooch. 2003. *Jjoeum ipsa* (*poamock ssanggum*). 24K gold wire, dot and sheet inlay on mild-steel plate, diamond settings, constructed, patina. 2.25" × 2" × 0.2".

조남우 (趙南宇) CHO Namu. *Mirage 9.* 2007. Brooch. 2003. *Jjoeum ipsa, tachul.* 24K gold wire, dot and sheet inlay on mild-steel plate, diamond settings, constructed, patina. 1.7" × 1.2" × 0.2".

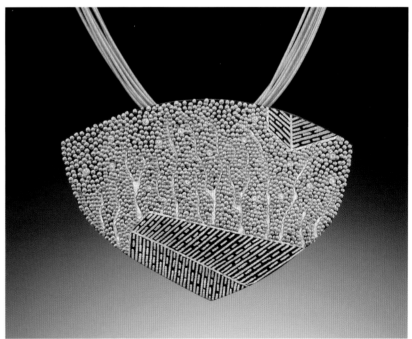

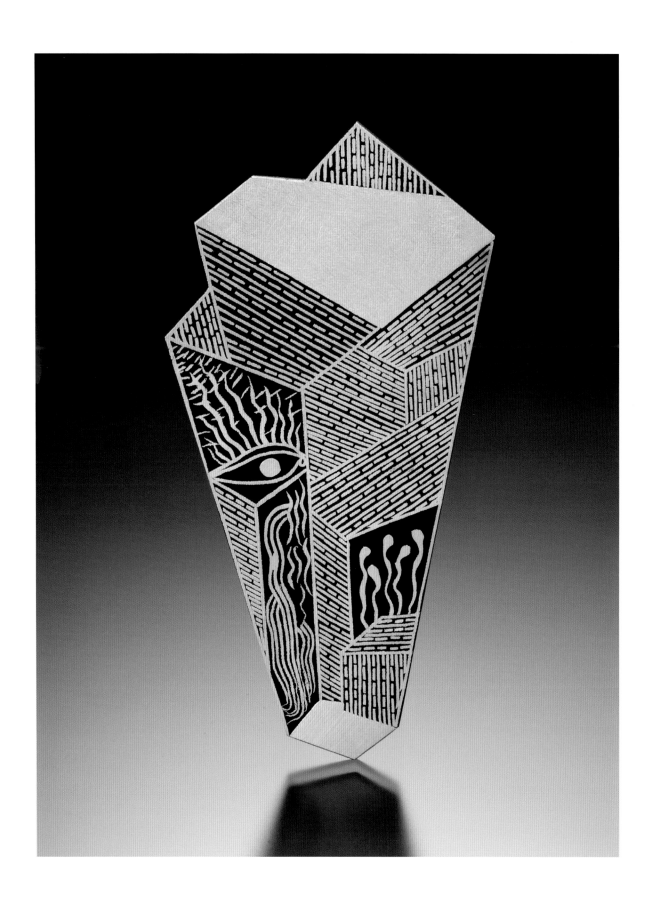

조남우 (趙南宇) CHO Namu.
Mirage 18. Brooch/pendant.
Poamock ssanggum (Korean
damascene), granulation (*nugeum*).
24K gold, steel. 3" × 2" × 0.5".

김성수 (金成洙) KIM Sungsoo.
King's Lake. Table. 2000. Iron, fine
silver, copper, 24K gold leaf (*keumpak*),
and *jjoeum ipsa.* 12" × 14" × 14".

The Chinese and Japanese hold
the dragon as their symbol of power,
but the Koreans' symbol of power is
represented by the holy mountain,
Baekdusan, and its lake, Cheonji.
This piece captures the majestic
clear and sacred water.

김성수 (金成洙) KIM Sungsoo.
King's Lake (close-up of handle
with *jjoeum ipsa*).

Since 1998, I have learned Korean techniques of *keum-boo* (24K gold overlay) and *poamock ssanggum* (*jjoeum ipsa*) from summer sessions led by Professor Komelia Okim at Southern Illinois University, Edwardsville. I had dedicated myself to drawing and painting before discovering the challenges and expressive potential within metalsmith art. *Jjoeum ipsa*, Korean-style damascene, allows me to indulge my fascination with sharp graphics of precious metals inlaid into dark, textile-like, hammer-chiseled mild-steel plates. Each piece begins with intense hammering and chiseling on mild steel, then transforms within partly chance-filled placement of 24K gold, fine-copper, and/or fine-silver wires (0.03 mm thick) and shapes to my wearable art jewelries.

COOL, Lynn. *Conduit 3, Emergent.* Ring. 2007. Hammer-chiseled on mild-steel plate, inlaid fine-silver patterns (*jjoeum ipsa*), colored, riveted to the hollow, constructed, and shaped sterling-silver ring. Sterling and fine silver, mild steel. 1.5" × 2.25" × 1".

COOL, Lynn. *Conduit 4, Ascension.* Pendant. 2007. Neck wire, hammer-chiseled on mild-steel plate, inlaid fine-silver and 24K gold wires and patterns (*jjoeum ipsa*), colored, set in to the constructed, shaped silver pendant with pearl and diamond settings. Sterling silver, 18K gold, 24K gold, mild steel, pearl, diamond. 3.5" × 1" × 1"; 22". *Courtesy of artist*

KANG Chan Kyun

강찬균 (姜燦均) KANG Chan Kyun, member of the National Academy of the Fine Arts in Metal Arts, the Republic of Korea. *Four Seasons*. Vessels. 1982. Dot and damascene inlays (*jjoeum ipsa*), formed, fabricated, and patina. Copper, 24K gold, fine silver. 9" × 4" × 4" each.

Two sets of containers convey warm family environments, using the traditional techniques but in contemporary expressions.

MYERS, Paulette

Myers's jewelry and holloware utilize Korean techniques of *jjoeum ipsa* and *keum-boo* as well as fabrication, forming, and reticulation as a vehicle to express the passage of time. Myers employs the *jjoeum ipsa* process to create a tapestry into time and space. The chiseled complex surface of parallel passes of cross-hatching creates the barbed canvas of rich, deep, blackened steel to capture the visually intense pure gold and silver foils and thin wires in an illusive layering of graphic portrayal. These objects, created in a medium of silver, gold, and iron, ensure their indestructibility and timelessness, while their embellishments of gemstones, coral, fossils, and pearls speak of the natural world.

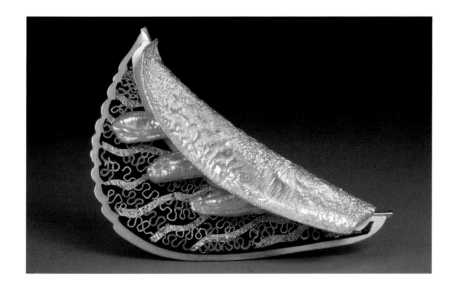

MYERS, Paulette. *Eternal Garden: Sea Spirit*. Brooch. 2005. *Jjoeum ipsa*, fabrication, forming, reticulation, piercing. Fine silver, sterling silver, 820 (reticulating) silver, 24K gold, mild steel, *biwa* pearls. 2.25" × 3.25" × 0.75".

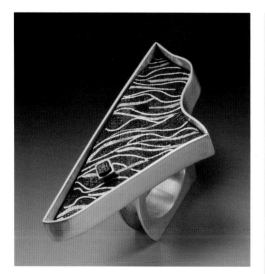

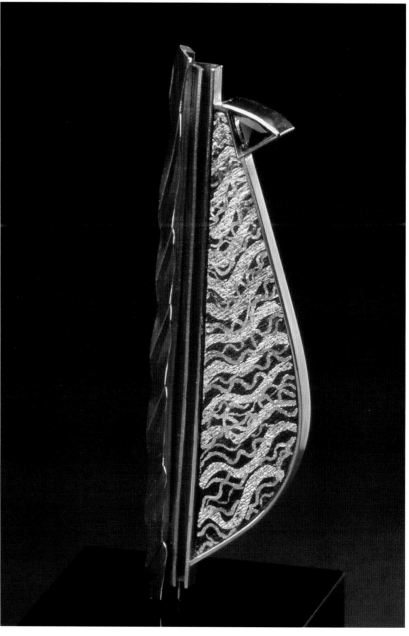

MYERS, Paulette. *Contemplation.* Ring. 2012. *Jjoeum ipsa*, fabrication, bezel setting. Argentium and fine silver, mild steel, 24K gold, 18K gold, raw diamond. 1.25" × 2.25" × 1.25".

Contemplation maps an ocean's journey through the Korean metal process of *jjoeum ipsa*, with waves of gold and silver embedded in chiseled, blackened mild steel.

MYERS, Paulette. *Illumination.* Brooch. 2010. *Jjoeum ipsa*, fabrication, piercing, reticulation, stone setting. Fine silver, sterling silver, 820 (reticulating) silver, mild steel, 24K gold, iolite. 3.75" × 1.75" × 0.5".

The traditional Korean techniques of *keum-boo* and *jjoeum ipsa* illuminate this regal cloaked figure.

LEE, Hannah Hyunah

Women in Asian countries lived in an environment of oppression and harassment. Yet, there is beauty and power in how they embraced their scars and lived in peace. Their emotions were invisible and hidden but were strong enough to shape life of themselves and others. I strive for these women to be brought out, visualized, and tangible to honor their bravery, faithfulness, perseverance, and contentment even in downcast situations. I used two Korean traditional techniques to express them in my work: *keum-boo* to reflect their temperate beauty, and *jjoeum ipsa* to contrast women's hope to their unchangeable situations.

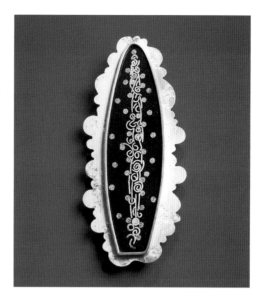

이현아 (李賢娥) LEE, Hannah Hyunah. *Starry, Starry Night.* Brooch. 2003. *Keum-boo, jjoeum ipsa.* Sterling silver, 24K gold and fine-silver inlay. 1.18" × 2.8" × 0.39".

WANG Lydia Hsia-Man

I used to look at the ocean from the mountain at midnight. The perfume bottle, titled *Mid-night Ocean*, reminds me of my hometown. In my work, the perfume bottle has become one of my favorite objects.

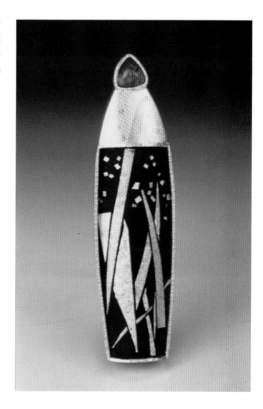

王夏滿 WANG Lydia Hsia-Man. *Memories.* Brooch. 2003. *Keum-boo, jjoeum ipsa.* Sterling silver, mild steel, 24K gold, and amber. 2.8" × 0.8" × 0.2".

LIN Chih-Yu Kevin

My work is both functional and sculptural. I explore the idea of containment by using images that surround us in everyday life: architecture, nature, and the figure. The contrast in a piece is important to me, whether it is the juxtaposition of the smooth surface against textured surface or the organic versus geometric form. I also take into consideration the different color variations of metal overlapping that finishes the piece.

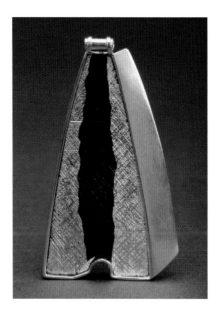

林致宇 LIN Chih-Yu Kevin. *Archway to My Memories.* Pendant. 2004. Korean-style damascene (*jjoeum ipsa*). Sterling silver, fine-silver foil, 24K gold foil, mild steel. 2.5" × 1.5" × 0.25".

JAUDÉS, Sherri

I use images from the insect and plant worlds to communicate emotions, events, and expressions from daily life. The various metal combinations and Korean techniques *keum-boo* and *jjoeum ipsa* add to the complexity of the overall design and help convey the story behind this work.

JAUDÉS, Sherri. *Emerging Life.* Necklace with locket. 2003. The colors of the beans are dramatized by the pattern of the *keum-boo* on the beetle's outer surface. Fabricated using sterling silver, fine silver, 24K gold foil, 18K gold, copper, patina, beans, and magnet. 17". *Photo, artist*

LONGYEAR, Robert

There is a question, a challenge, and a resolution that draw forward a facsimile of the landscape of the made but make it manageable, comprehensible, and sometimes small, so that you feel the sense of the individual maker, manipulator, a personality out in the world transforming it.

LONGYEAR, Robert. *Malaya.* Brooch. 2003. *Jjoeum ipsa.* Mild steel, sterling silver, fine silver, and 24K gold. 2.5" × 3.25 × .75". *Photo, artist*

ZUMBRO, Leia

ZUMBRO, Leia. *Budding.* Pendant as locket. 2007. Hand fabricated, Korean-style damascene setting, oxidized, locket with hinges and opening mechanism. 24K gold foil, fine-silver foil, mild steel, brass, steel cable necklace. 2.25" × 1" × 1"; 20".

ZUMBRO was inspired by watching the budding of a blooming of flowers. *Budding* was made as a locket to show the opening of a bud, while the brass leaves encircle the steel to close it. The damascene technique inlay (*jjoeum ipsa*) was used to inlay 24K gold foil shapes to emulate the flecks on flowers. The steel was then blackened all over and sporadically rusted to further enforce the organic look of the piece.

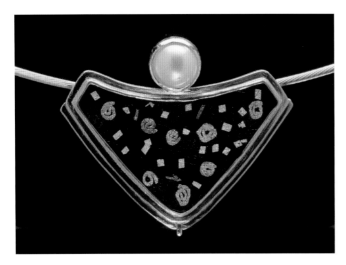

HUNG, Angela K. *Moonlight I.* Pendant. 2004. Hand fabricated, damascene (*jjoeum ipsa*) setting, oxidized. 24K gold, gold foil (*keum-boo*), silver foil *(eunpak)*, fine silver, sterling silver, mild steel, freshwater pearl. 1.5" × 0.5" × 0.5"; 22".

HUNG was inspired by the Chinese poem "Quiet Night Thoughts" by the Tang-dynasty poet Li Bai. The poem describes the longing and feelings of homesickness while gazing at the night's moon through a window. The artist used large freshwater pearls, representing the moon, atop a simple triangle as light radiates from the moon. The Korean damascene technique (*jjoeum ipsa*) was used to inlay shapes made of gold and silver foils and oxidized, and set pearl damascene inlay.

TENEBAUM, Joan

TENEBAUM, Joan. *Foggy Woman: A Dena'ina Story.* Brooch. 2007. Damascene (*jjoeum ipsa*), roll printing, fabricated, 24K gold overlay (*keum-boo*), piercing, carving, riveting, patina. Sterling silver, mild steel, 24K gold, 14K gold, and copper. 2.5" × 2.125" × 0.25". *Photo, Doug Yaple*

My work and my life are a continuous journey. In hand-fabricated pieces, I tell stories and paint pictures of the peoples with whom I lived in the Far North, and of places of transcendent beauty. These are wearable miniature landscapes with both cultural themes and ecological messages.

HOWARD-CLINGER, Aimee

When I was first introduced to the technique of *jjoeum ipsa*, I was intrigued by the process's ability to elevate steel to that of a precious metal through surface transformation and inlay. Traditionally, steel is associated with industrial applications rather than jewelry. However, through the process of *jjoeum ipsa*, the steel becomes an imperative component for the decorative surface to exist.

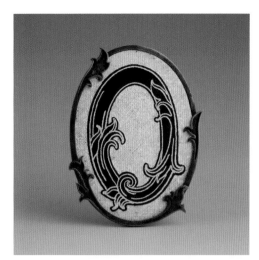

HOWARD-CLINGER, Aimee. *Ornamental Brooch.* Brooch. 2017. Fine-silver wire inlaid onto chiseled mild-steel sheet metal (*jjoeum ipsa)* then back-set into fabricated and oxidized silver frame. Fine silver and steel. 3" × 2" × 0.25". *Courtesy of artist*

MADDOX, Jan

As an artist, I loved the fact that I could use not only the colors of gold and silver together, but also the richness of the black mild-steel backgrounds in abstract designs. I set those Korean damascene-style inlays (*jjoeum ipsa*) into my jewelry-like jewels with stitching, setting, and riveting.

MADDOX, Jan. *Damascene Quarter Circle #4.* Brooch. 1990. Korean-style damascene (*jjoeum ipsa*) and 24K gold overlay (*keum-boo*). Mild steel, sterling silver, 24K gold, orange sapphire, hematite. 3" × 3.25" × 0.25". *Photo, David Terao*

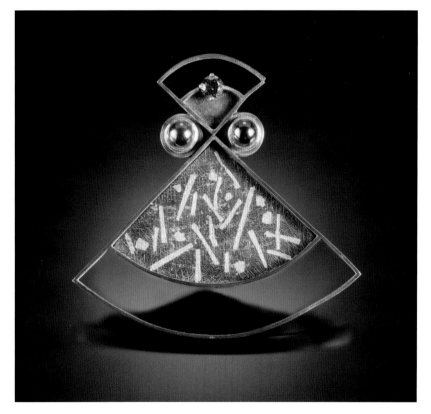

MADDOX, Jan. *Damascene Loup.*
Brooch. 1989. Korean-style
damascene (*jjoeum ipsa*) and 24K
gold overlay (*keum-boo*). Mild
steel, sterling silver, 14K gold, 24K
gold, hematite. 2" × 1.75" × 0.25".
Photo, David Terao

TYSON CHOI, Mira

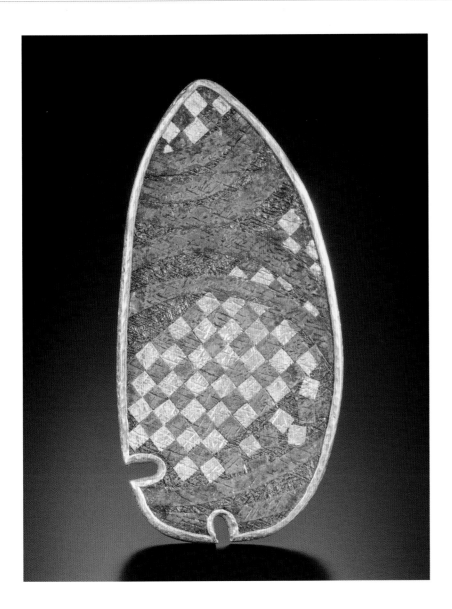

TYSON CHOI, Mira. *Impression of Native American Arrowheads I.* Brooch. 1991. *Jjoeum ipsa* and oxidation. Mild steel, fine and sterling silver, copper. 2" × 1.5" × 0.5". Nearly three decades ago, I received my first impression of Native American arrowheads. I was highly impressed by the rough edges, simple lines, and variations in shape. This work, inspired by my experiences, uses a traditional Korean metal surface technique in conjunction with my imagination of the life of the people who created these arrowheads.

윤정화 (尹正和) YOON Jungwha. *Landscape 1*. Brooch. 1991. *Kkium ipsa*, *jjoeum ipsa*, *keum-boo*, roll printing, hydraulic forming, fabricating, 24K gold inlaying, setting, and patina. Fine and sterling silver, mild steel, 24K gold foil. 3" × 3.5" × 0.5".

윤정화 (尹正和) YOON Jungwha. *Landscape 2*. Brooch. 1991. *Jjoeum ipsa*, *keum-boo*, roll printing, hydraulic forming, fabricating, 24K gold inlaying, setting, and patina. Fine and sterling silver, mild steel, 24K gold foil. 3" × 3" × 0.5".

Yoon Jungwha's Brooch series portrays Korean landscapes created with *jjoeum ipsa* and *keum-boo* techniques. Traditional 24K gold overlay was used for spoons reserved for special occasions. The artist uses traditional techniques as a way of wishing special blessings and experiences for those wearing her brooches.

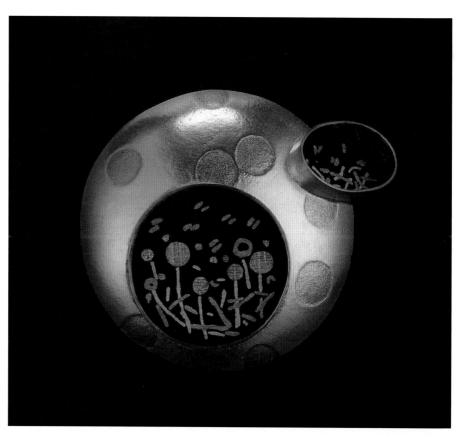

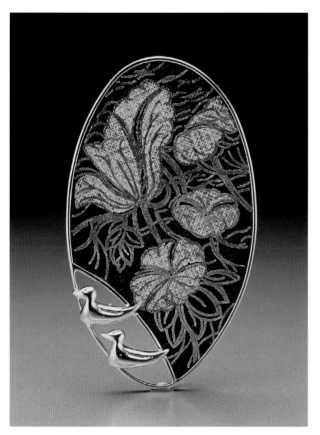

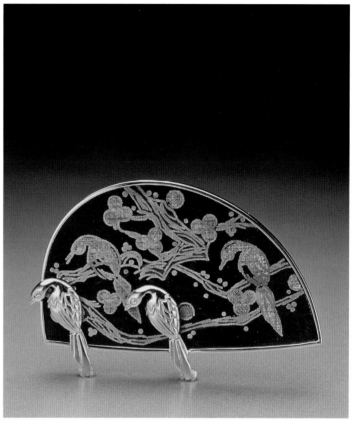

조유진 (曺有珍) CHO Yujin. *Once upon a Time IX*. Brooch. 2006. *Jjoeum ipsa*. 24K gold, 18K gold, fine silver, steel. 2.7" × 1.6" × 0.4". Inspired by Korean traditional folk painting, I presented the lotus leaves with Korean inlay technique. A pictorial pair of lovebirds looking in one direction symbolizes a future-oriented partnership. With the contrast of the darkness of base metal, it delivers the feeling of my own drawing.

조유진 (曺有珍) CHO Yujin. *Once upon a Time VII*. Brooch. 2006. *Jjoeum ipsa*. 24K gold, fine silver, 18K gold, steel. 2" × 2.7" × 0.4". Presenting the flowers in full bloom on a spring day by overlapping a plain bird and one in half relief, I wanted to create interesting perspectives and aesthetic qualities.

YOO Lizzy (1945–2013)

유리지 (劉里知) YOO Lizzy. *Evening Stroll*. Object. 1986. Raising, forming, casting, chasing and repoussé (*tachul*), marriage of metals (*jeoul ipsa*), Korean damascene technique (*jjoeum ipsa*), and line inlay (*kkium ipsa*). Sterling silver, nickel silver, brass, iron, patina. 5.5" × 13.8" × 9.4". *Collection of Yoo Lizzy Metal Crafts Museum*

In *Evening Stroll*, the two oval shapes represent the moon and clouds, depicting an image of evening wonder. The scene is executed with imagination and fantasy.

유리지 (劉里知) YOO Lizzy.
Looking at a Hill. Kettle and tray.
1987. Raising, forming, marriage of
metals (*jeoul ipsa*), chasing and
repoussé (*tachul*), line inlay (*kkium
ipsa*), 24K gold overlay (*keum-boo*),
and riveting. Sterling silver, nickel
silver, iron, 24K gold, ivory, patina.
8.8" × 14" × 9.6". *Collection of
Yoo Lizzy Metal Crafts Museum*
   Looking at a Hill forms the
voluminous shape of cloud into a
body and a lid for a pot, with the
shape of grass depicting a hill that
is stretched long to become a
design of a handle. In this work,
the artist uses *keum-boo* (24K gold
overlay) technique and, with the
oldest traditional metalcraft
techniques, achieves both
practicality and aesthetic quality of
the time. In this period Yoo was
also interested in combining
realistic shapes into geometrically
stylized shapes, selecting subjects
such as flowers and fishes for the
theme of her works.

Hammer-Chasing-Engraving (*Jjoi Ipsa*)

The traditional technique of *jangseok* used this hammer-chasing-engraving method on all metal surfaces, including added corner elements. The corner elements, sectional hinging parts, and locks on items such as furniture, boxes, and mirror stands added longevity. This technique is similar to hand engraving but with the use of a hammer; deeper lines can be chiseled to emphasize elaborate designs on brass or white- or yellow-nickel surfaces.

**Historical References:
Museum Collections**

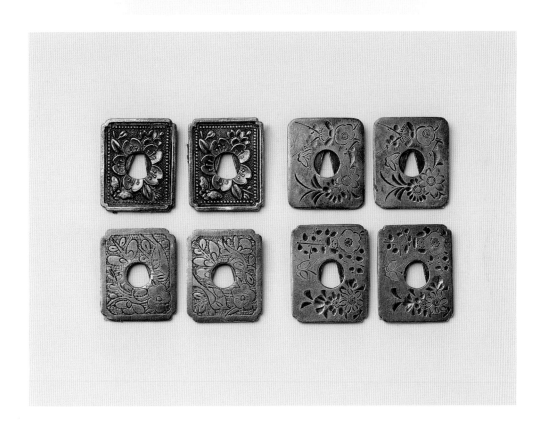

Previous page: Flame Ewer & Basin. No. GM 223. Goryeo dynasty, eleventh–thirteenth centuries. *Jjoi ipsa* and *tachul*. Gold-plated silver. 14.8" × 8.8" × 6.16"; 7.04" × 7.28" × 7.28". *Collection of Cheonmisa*

Hunting Scene. No. GM 168. Small jar. Three Kingdoms period, third–fourth centuries. *Jjoi ipsa* (hammer-chasing-engraving) and *jangseok*. Iron, gold-plating sections. 4.3" × 3.6". *Collection of Cheonmisa*

Danchu. No. 085. Men's buttons made of silver. Joseon dynasty, twentieth century. 0.7"–0.9". *Sookmyung Women's University Museum*

Three Norigae Pendants. No. 073-1.
Personal ornaments without hanging
tassels. Joseon dynasty, 1392–1897
CE. Silver with surface *Jjoi ipsa* and
jangseok. 0.8"–2.6". *Sookmyung
Women's University Museum*

Pendants represent a peach
and a plum flower; fish, and a
boy's pouches; these hang on the
belt and are believed to bring
wealth and prosperity of the
family, as well as long life. These
are used among upper-class
women's personal ornaments.

Jangdo Norigae. No. 78. Pendant
knives. Joseon dynasty, 1392–1897
CE.

These ornamental knife pendants
are made with silver and were used
as a self-defense weapon for
married women, being presented as
wedding gifts from the groom's
family. The knife edge is made of
strong steel. Enameling, silver, steel,
coral. 3" × 3" × 0.5". *Sookmyung
Women's University Museum*

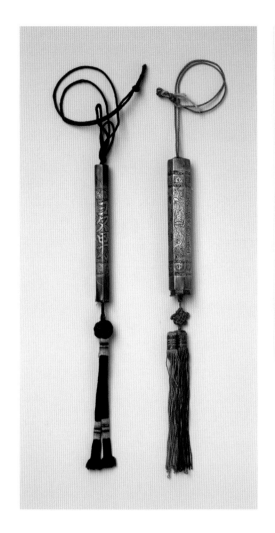

Chimtong Suncho. No. 058.
Pendants with needle cases. Joseon
dynasty, twentieth century.
14.7"–15.0". *Sookmyung Women's
University Museum*
   These pendants are for
acupuncture needle cases; made
with silver for utilitarian purposes
and as decorative objects and
used as central parts of everyday
use for traveling.

Sam-Jack Norigae. No. 2407.
Three Norigae pendants with
shapes of Tuho (Game of arrows
pitching into a pot). Joseon
dynasty, nineteenth century. Coral,
pearl, and three-color silk tassel of
Korean macramé for royal officer's
family; the top pendant has the
design of peony in the square
frame. 15.75". Has a meaning of
long life, luck, and health. *Jjoi ipsa,
jangseok. Seokjuseon Memorial
Dankook University Museum*

Ssang-Garakji. No. 145. Double rings. Nineteenth century. These double rings are worn only among married women. These are decorated with only hammer-chisel-engraving designs and are worn among lower-class women. Silver. 0.8"–1.4". *Collection of Ewha Woman's University Museum, CHANG Pudeok Memorial Gallery*

Lock with Bosangwha Patterns. Late Joseon dynasty, nineteenth century. Overlapping and transforming lotus flower patterns representing nirvana in Buddhism. Nickel. 4.3" × 2.1" × 1.1". *Lock Museum*

Gilt Silver Basin & Ewer. No.
35.646a–b. Goryeo dynasty, twelfth
century. Parcel gilt silver with
engraved decoration (*jjoi ipsa*).
13.5" × 3.75"; 6.7" × 7.52" × 5.8".
*Photograph © 2018, Museum of
Fine Arts, Boston*

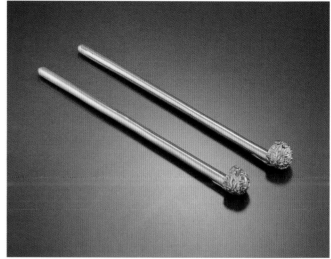

Chrysanthemum Box. Goryeo dynasty, 918–1392 CE. 1.9" × 1.2". *Tokyo National Museum*

Peony Pattern Long Hair Sticks. Nos. 094, 095. Joseon dynasty (early twentieth century). *National Palace Museum*

Silver Box and Gilt-Bronze Box. Reliquary. Hwangnyongsa Temple site. Silla dynasty, eighth–ninth centuries. 1.75" × 2.875". *National Museum of Korea*

Cosmetics Jar. Joseon dynasty, 1650 CE. No. 58-1. Silver. 2.53". *National Museum of Korea*

CHO Sung-joon

KOREAN INTANGIBLE CULTURAL PROPERTY NO.
260 MASTER CRAFTSPERSON

CHO Sung-joon is a master craftsperson
using traditional techniques to form replicas
for museums, incorporating his own contemporary approaches.

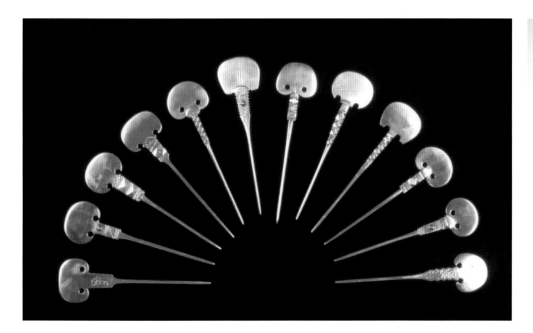

조성준 (趙聖濬) CHO Sung-joon.
Korea Intangible Cultural Property
No. 260: *Jjoi Ipsa* Master
Craftsperson and Practitioner.
Various shapes of *bichigae*.
Ornaments. 1992. These types of
hair ornaments were used as
cleaning combs. They were also
used to part hair, or simply as hair
ornaments. Nickel, yellow brass.

조성준 (趙聖濬) CHO Sung-joon.
Korea Intangible Cultural Property
No. 260: *Jjoi Ipsa* Master
Craftsperson and Practitioner.
*Square Brazier & Fire-Picking
Chopsticks*. Charcoal burner. 1993.
Carving, constructing, joinery,
odong, jjoeum ipsa, keum-boo.
Nickel, red brass, yellow brass,
copper, *odong*, 24K gold. 6" × 6" ×
6.4"; 11.2".
    This portable charcoal burner, or
hwaro, was used inside the
enclosed hand-carried royal carrier,
gama, during winter months. This
square brazier is a replica of the
historical object, made with
identical design, materials, and
traditional techniques.

조성혜 (趙星慧) CHO Sung Hae.
Dream of Millennium. Vessel. 2010.
Jjoi ipsa, raising, forming,
fabricating, line inlaying (*kkium
ipsa*), and patina. Iron, fine silver,
copper, and nitro-coloring. 5.1" ×
5.1" × 5.1".

조성혜 (趙星慧) CHO Sung Hae. *Wedding Day Box.* Vessel. 2007. *Jjoi ipsa* and *jeoul ipsa.* Iron, fine silver, copper, and black *odong* 8% gold. 3.9" × 3.9" × 3.9".

LIM Ock Soo

This jar was created by cylinder tub-raising, forming, and constructing by welding. It features deep electro-etched traditional patterns of fish and flowers, which were inlayed with thick wire and grounded a little higher than the background to make the patterns more prominent (*jjoeum ipsa* and *odong ipsa*).

임옥수 (林玉洙) LIM Ock Soo. *Hangarii* (Top view).

임옥수 (林玉洙) LIM Ock Soo. *Hangarii.* Large jar with lid. 1994. Copper, patina. 22.5" × 18" × 16.5".

The Korean traditional ceramic moon-shaped jar design inspired the production of these silver vessels. *Jjoeum ipsa, kkium ipsa*, and *keum-boo* techniques add volume, serenity, richness, and beautifully contrasting colors of silver and gold.

Process for *Incense Burner 2*

First create the container. Embellish the design areas with line and shape inlay techniques by using 24K gold foils and wires. Apply heat from the bottom of the vessel for the 24K gold overlay *keum-boo* process. Outline the *keum-boo* areas by adding *jjoi ipsa* (hammer chasing engraving) that looks like stitched outlines.

Lightly hammer over the designs with an iron rod (like planishing) to make sure the gold shapes and lines are applied evenly on the silver bowl, without any raised areas or air bubbles. The lid is plated with 24K gold.

정양희 (鄭良姬) JUNG Yanghee. *Incense Burner No. 2*. Container. 1995. Raising, forming, planishing, line inlaying, Korean damascene, fusing with 24K gold overlay finish; *jjoeum ipsa, kkium ipsa, keum-boo*. Silver, 24K gold. 7.5" × 7" × 7.5".

Incense Burner No. 2 has a high-domed lid that is 24K-gold-plated to accomplish strong contrast between the bowl and lid.

정양희 (鄭良姬) JUNG Yanghee. *Vessel No. 2*. Container. 1995. Raising, forming, planishing, line inlaying, Korean damascene, fusing with 24K gold overlay finish; *jjoeum ipsa, kkium ipsa, keum-boo*. Silver, 24K gold. 5.5" × 5.5" × 7".

Process for Making *Feast of Butterflies 2*

Raising-forming technique was used to create volumes and consistent patterns on the surface with the hammer-created pattern for texturing. The pitch is filled, to emphasize the volume, shape, and details, with *jjoeum ipsa*, *kkium ipsa*, and *jjoi ipsa* filled with fine-silver foil and wire inlays to emphasize the defined shape and outlining of images. The front and back parts are welded and finished. Potassium sulfide is used for coloring, and verdigris is applied for patina. Finally, beeswax is polished lightly onto the heated surface with soft cloths.

김현준 (金顯晙) KIM Hyun Jun.
Feast of Butterflies 2. Object. 2009.
Jjoeum ipsa, kkium ipsa inlay
techniques, raising, forming,
hammer patterned-texturing.
Copper, silver, fine silver foil, wire
and patina. 5" × 23" × 15".

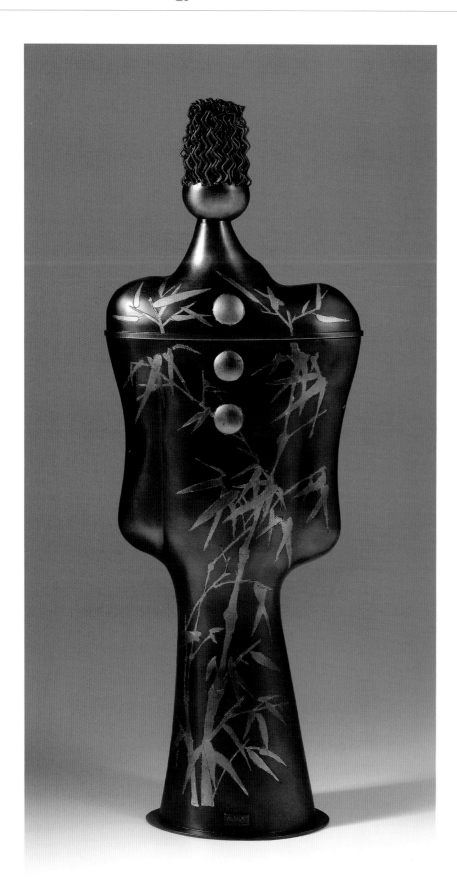

김홍자 (金弘子) OKIM Komelia Hongja. *Godfather.* Memory container. 2015–2017. Sinking forming, curled-wire soldered, fabricating, hammer-chisel-engraving (*jjoi ipsa*), *keum-boo* overlaying, oxidizing and highlighting, and sumac clear lacquering (*jjoi ipsa*, *keum-boo*, and *ottchil*). Fine and sterling silver, 24K gold *keum-boo*. 20" × 17.5" × 4.5".

This container is for the funerary vessel for keeping ashes or memorabilia. The vessel has three Korean traditional techniques of *jjoi ipsa*, *keum-boo*, and *ottchil* for surface decorations, and application of *ottchil* inside and outside for preservation and to prevent discolorations.

Black-Crow Color Inlay (*Odong Ipsa*)

Odong ipsa uses metal alloys of 8–10 percent pure gold and 80 percent white nickel or copper, with chiseled-out patterns that are filled with solder. It is the white solder inlay on black-crow metal background that is called *odong ipsa*.

Historically, these methods were used during the Goryeo dynasty on *jangseok* (joinery) decorating units in wooden furniture and traditional gate locks.

This method became a well-developed and popular one during the Joseon dynasty for use on *dambedae*, long tobacco pipes. These tobacco pipes were usually used among noble upper-class men who wanted to show their status. The pipe had a long, black bamboo handle with a nickel mouthpiece, and the bowl section would contain tobacco. The pipes often feature checkerboard patterns of contrasting black-and-white color. Typically, 70 percent silver solder was used to get the black color effect in the smaller sections with linear patterns.

The entire surface of these deep-cut patterns was filled with the solder inlay method to get the best effect. After flooding the whole surface with solder, the surface was filed to make it even. To get a black patina, the patina was tightly wrapped in rice paper and dipped into stale urine, then left in sunlight. This process of oxidizing by using stale urine with ammonia and the heat from the sun turns the metal black. Deer skin was used to burnish the object after coloring to add a luster finish.

Contemporary Korean artists now use ammonia substitutes to obtain a similar effect, but the color is not as deep as one would obtain through traditional methods. They use a cotton swab dipped in ammonia to slowly paint the surface until the desired black color is achieved.

Historical References: Museum Collections

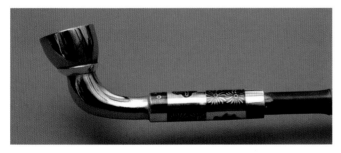

황영보 HWANG Young-bo, Intangible Cultural Heritage No. 65: *Baekdong Yeonjukjang* Holder. *White Nickel Long Odong Pipe.* No. 29366. 2006. Nickel, copper with 8% gold, black-crow metal, bamboo. Close-up of frontal tobacco container of the long pipe. *Odong ipsa* (black-crow color inlay). *National Intangible Cultural Heritage Center (The Art of Tobacco-Pipe Making)*

황영보 HWANG Young-bo, Intangible Cultural Heritage No. 65: *Baekdong Yeonjukjang* Holder. *White Nickel Long Odong Pipe.* No. 29366. Nickel, copper with 8% gold, black-crow metal, bamboo. Close-up of middle section of the long pipe. *Odong ipsa* (black-crow color inlay). *National Intangible Cultural Heritage Center (The Art of Tobacco-Pipe Making)*

Traditional Nobleman's Smoking Pipe Demonstration by KIM Seung Hee (Followed Master TCHU Jeong-Ryeol's *Odong Ipsa* Method)

Throughout the nineteenth-century Joseon dynasty (1892–1897), noblemen enjoyed smoking from long, elegant pipes called *odong yeonsoock* made of *odong ipsa* (copper alloy with 8%–10% gold alloy) and black bamboo.

Odong (crow copper) is an alloy of 8–10 percent gold and 80 percent copper that is finished to a deep-black color by wrapping the piece in stale-urine-saturated rice paper and left on a glass sheet for several hours under the sun. Metalsmiths today substitute ammonia for stale urine. White-nickel alloy is composed of 58 percent copper, 37 percent nickel, and 5 percent gold alloy.

1. Prepare materials:

   1 copper sheet (1.4" × 1.5", 22 gauge)

   2 fine-silver sheets (0.6" × 0.7", 30 gauge)

   2 fine-silver sheets (0.3" × 0.7", 30 gauge)

   2 *odong* sheets (0.6" × 0.7", 30 gauge)

   2 *odong* sheets (0.3" × 0.7", 30 gauge)

Traditional nobleman's smoking pipe made by Master TCHU Jeong-Ryeol (1927–1991).

Clean all nine sheets in an acid bath, rinse, and dry.

Cover the entire surface of metal sheets with Borax flux (borax powder boiled slowly in water while grinding until the powder is very fine and the consistency of Handy-flux paste) and allow to dry.

Place copper, fine-silver, and *odong* sheets in a checkerboard pattern as shown.

2. Use iron clips to hold base metal and checkerboard metals together.

3. Place square chips of solder (70% fine silver, 10% zinc; similar to hard solder) in the middle of the joints, as shown. Solder the checkerboard to the base metal.

4. Prepare *odong* design patterns. Punch out the *odong* patterns (30-gauge thin sheet) to be soldered onto the fine silver with a sharp die. Use the same die and a chasing hammer to make shaped dents in the fine-silver squares.

5. Put flux in the indented areas in the fine silver and allow it to dry. Melt solder onto the back of the cutout *odong* pattern pieces and place them into the indentations in the fine silver. Solder in place, being careful to keep flux off the *odong* patterns so that solder will not jump onto the top of the piece.

Use a scraper or file to file off excess solder on the soldered surfaces.

After pickling and cleaning the piece, place it on a lead block and flatten the front surface with a rawhide mallet, keeping strikes light. The back side of the plate will look a little thicker because of the inlay. File the back side until flat and finish smoothly with light hammer blows to even the sheet of the metal.

6. Apply linear patterns according to the design with cutting-chasing tool and light chasing hammer.

7. Chisel the designs with cutting-chasing tool and hammer. Flux the chiseled designs and allow them to dry. Place small chips of solder, and heat to flow the solder into the chiseled indentations. After pickling and rinsing, examine the piece carefully to make sure that all design areas are filled with solder, and that the seams are well soldered and filed (to achieve solder inlay).

Create a cylindrical tube from the sheet.

8. Go over the entire surface of the tube to check soldered seams.

9. Prepare the surface for application. Traditionally, this involves filing from coarse to medium to fine, and polishing with diamond polishing stones. The final polishing is done with the finest compound and cloth by hand for a mirror finish.

Master TCHU used the old technique of blackening *odong*, by wrapping the *torii* (tobacco pipe handle area with *odong*-patterned section) area in Korean rice paper, *hanji*, soaking it in stale urine and placing it on a sheet of glass in sunlight for three to four hours. This gives a black-purple color to the *odong*, creating a strong contrast with the fine-silver and solder inlay in the checkerboard patchwork patterns.

Traditional craftspeople (and masters) use *odong* inlay patterns of pear flowers, cranes, and clouds to symbolize nature and longevity.

Square Series of Brooches Made with *Odong Ipsa* Technique with Contemporary Approaches by KIM Seung Hee

KIM Seung Hee's work uses traditional techniques to produce contemporary designs in the Square Jewelry series. On the Hill I & II Container series is first sketched and then executed on the works, using the *odong ipsa* technique.

Kim used square application of *odong* demonstration, as in *torii* sections of the pipe in creating a flat 2-D application, but created a 3-D effect as seen in the *odong ipsa* tobacco pipe methods. Kim used a graphic effect by using *odong* coloring methods to create a 2-D surface with 3-D effects.

1. Prepare tools for *odong ipsa*: punches, square cutting punches, pitch, vise, chasing hammers.
2. Prepare 16-gauge fine silver and prepared *odong* sheet of 1.4" × 1.4".
3. Place *odong* sheet on the lead block and hammer the square indentations, using a heavy chasing hammer. Hammer square, sharp, chasing-punch shapes to the fine-silver plate on the lead block, which shows convex bumps on the backplate.
4. Prepare to add linear design by hammer-chisel-cut lines: place a wood block in the vise and melt pitch onto the wooden block.
5. Prepare a thin *odong* plate (22 gauge) and punch out the square shapes of *odong* that will be inserted into the square dents in the fine-silver sheet.
6. Point torch flame to attach the *odong* squares and allow solder to flow in the chiseled line grooves (the solder is an alloy of 70% fine silver, 20% copper, and 10% zinc). The solder will melt to fill all seams of the back piece (solder inlay).
7. Clean well in an acid bath to remove all flux and surface oxidation.
8. File down the square bumps so that they are flush with the backing sheet of metal. It is important to file the *odong ipsa* flat to make sure that the solder inlay looks very sharp. This ensures that the final coloring of *odong ipsa* will have a sharp contrast between black-and-white background color.
9. Flatten the sheet by using a medium chasing hammer carefully, to avoid distorting the overall shape of the piece. Create a 14K gold frame by using 0.03" × 0.07" square wire and solder the square *odong ipsa* work.
10. Polish on the polishing wheel.
11. Finished work is soaked in a solution made from dissolving a small amount of liquid soap and 3 tablespoons of caustic soda in 2 liters of warm water at 68°F (20°C). Soak until the desired color develops. Color will change from pale red to purple, deep purple, greenish blue, blue, brown, and finally black. For black color development, leave the work in the solution for one to three hours.
12. Rinse completed work with clean water and buff with a clean cloth. The colors of this piece range from deep blue to various shades of plum.

김승희 (金昇姬) KIM Seung Hee.
Mountain Series I, II, III, IV.
Brooches. 1981. *Odong ipsa.*
Odong, sterling silver, 70% silver
solder, and 14K gold frame. 1.4" ×
1.2" × 0. 5" each.

김승희 (金昇姫) KIM Seung Hee. *Hillside with a Horizontal Line 1 & 2*. Containers. 1982. *Odong ipsa.* Copper, brass, nickel silver, crow copper, and 70% silver solder. 6.4" × 6.4" × 2.8"; 5.1" × 5.1" × 5.5".

김승희 (金昇姫) KIM Seung Hee. *Three Pendants and Earrings.* 2016. *Odong ipsa. Odong*, 18K gold, pearl, and patina. 0.5" × 5" × 5.9"; 18".

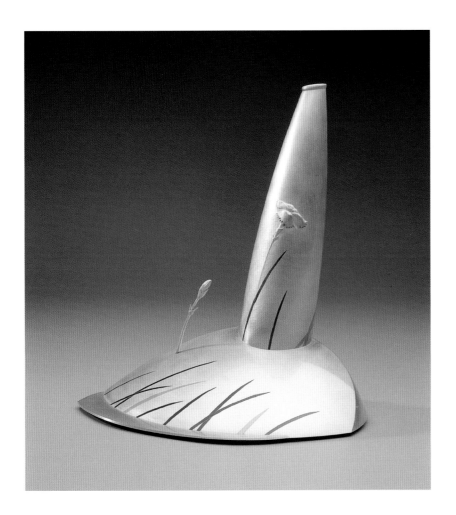

유리지 (劉里知) YOO Lizzy.
Leaning on the Wind. Vase. 1987.
Raising, forming, chasing and
repoussé (*tachul*), line inlay (*kkium
ipsa*), marriage of metals (*jeoul
ipsa*), 24K gold overlay (*keum-boo*).
Sterling silver, nickel silver, 24K
gold, *odong*, patina. 10.12" × 9" ×
6.6". *Collection of Yoo Lizzy Metal
Crafts Museum*

YOO Lizzy produced the flower
vase *Leaning on the Wind* to feel
the difference between an object
and an artwork with function. By
presenting artworks that modern-
ized the traditional Korean funeral
culture in 2000, she firmly
expanded the practicality of craft
and the possibility of formative
expression that crosses over the
border of aesthetics.

Marriage of Metals (*Jeoul Ipsa*)

Marriage of metals (*jeoul ipsa*) is a technique that produces a flat sheet of metal formed from two to three layers of different-colored metals. Traditional marriage of metals from the Three Kingdoms period (fourth to fifth centuries) was used to show distinctive designs wherever the metal was carved. This technique can be seen among locks for large door handles and special boxes used in the royal courts.

Throughout the era of the nineteenth-century Joseon dynasty, special locks can be seen in *Taeguk* (center shape in the Korean flag) patterns symbolizing the balance between negative yin energy and positive yang energy (*Eum* and *Yang* dualities). Marriage of metals is used to show strong contrast of the patterns for expressing meanings or to show contrasting designs.

Historical References: Museum Collections

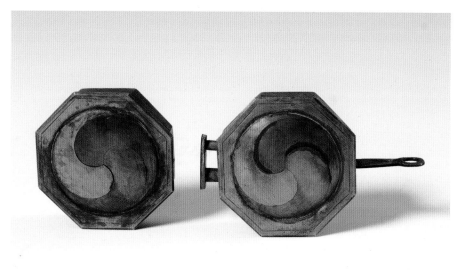

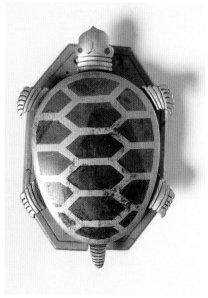

Drum-Shaped Lock. Late Joseon dynasty, twentieth century. Nickel, copper, and brass. *Taeguk* patterns symbolize the basic principle of the universe (yin and yang) and fortune. 1" × 4.3" × 4.3". *Lock Museum*

Turtle-Shaped Lock. Late Joseon dynasty, twentieth century. Marriage of metals (*jeoul ipsa*). Nickel, silver, brass, and copper. This symbolizes long life and protection. 0.4" × 3.2" × 4.4". *Lock Museum*

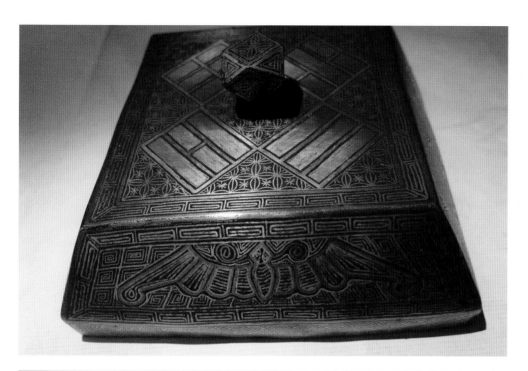

Iron Brazier. No. 2606. Joseon dynasty, 1392–1910 CE. *Jeoul ipsa* (marriage of metals), inlaid with silver and copper wire. Iron, silver, copper. 8.4". *National Museum of Korea*

Iron Tray. Joseon dynasty, 1392–1897 CE. *Jeoul ipsa* and *kkium ipsa* (marriage of metals and line inlay). Iron, silver, copper. 14.2". *National Museum of Korea*

Marriage of Metals (*Jeoul Ipsa*)
Demonstration by KANG Heewon for
Multicolored Brooches

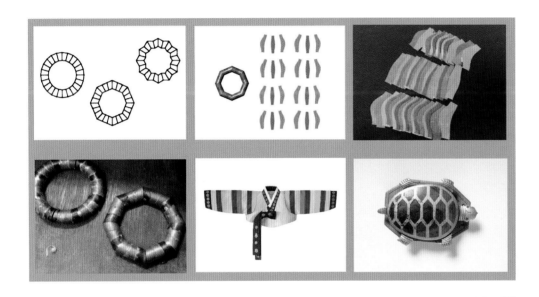

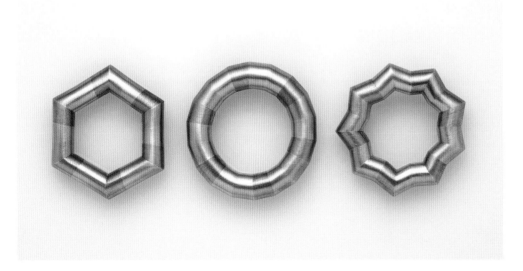

강희원 (康熹元) KANG Heewon.
Multicolored I, II, III. Brooches.
2016. Marriage of metals (*jeoul
ipsa*). Copper, brass, nickel silver.
0.5" × 2.3" × 2.3" each.

Marriage of Metals (*Jeoul Ipsa*) Process by JUNG Young Kuwan

I wanted to create a boundary line that looked more natural after sawing. After repeated experiments of inlaid work, I found a technique that achieves this more natural-looking border.

Materials:

copper and red brass rods 0.1" × 16"–20" (0.3 cm × 40–50 cm long), 2–3 different color metals

    Measure the width wanted. (Example: 18" width wanted, 18" ÷ 0.1" = 180; therefore 180 rods are needed)

powder flux (use for casting): Make sure the powder is well ground. Mix with distilled water. Cook slowly and stir well until finely mixed.

wide flux brush

flat sheets of soldering board (flat hard ceramic kiln shelves)

natural gas or propane and oxygen torch

Process:

1. Alternate placing copper and brass rods (and/or nickel) for marriage of metals.

2. Cover the entire surface of the rods with prepared flux.

3. Using big torch flames, heat slowly until the fluxed surface is clearly melted and glassy.

4. Make sure the rods have no gaps between them with big stainless-steel tweezers, and start adding hard copper-wire solder (or hard silver-wire solder) from one end until all rods are well soldered.

5. Solder the rods, making sure there are no gaps in between them.

6. Decide how much to solder the length of rods on both ends.

7. Place the whole soldered structure into the large bath to pickle.

8. Using a wide rolling mill, thin the structure slowly to desired thickness by annealing in between the plate.

9. Use the newly formed *jeoul ipsa* plate for desired project.

10. *Jeoul ipsa* (marriage of metals) sheet used for raising vessels.

JUNG Young Kuwan

정영관 (鄭永琯) JUNG Young Kuwan. *Field at Dusk*. Container. 1991. Marriage of metals (*jeoul ipsa*). Copper, brass, nickel. 22" × 16" × 8".

The inlaid work within the plate maximizes the natural feeling of the boundary lines. When the plate is rolled without soldering both sides, an organic branch-shaped pattern comes out. This technique works to more effectively increase the lyricism that I have as a recurring theme in my work.

Process for *Bracelet #15* by KIM Shin-Lyoung

Jeoul ipsa (marriage of metals) with fine silver and nickel silver creates many different shades of blacks by heat coloring.

1. Draw design on nickel silver and saw out areas to be filled with fine silver. Finish the edges and surfaces with files and sandpaper.
2. Insert fine-silver inlay pieces (0.1–0.2 mm thicker than the nickel plate) into the sawed-out areas of the nickel plate.
3. Use hard solder with gas and compressed-air or acetylene torches with #3 to #5 tips (not gas/oxygen or oxygen/acetylene torches) to join fine silver to the nickel.
4. Finish soldering the bracelet, using medium and easy solder.
5. Color the bracelet by heat coloring, which blackens the nickel and accentuates the fine-silver design.

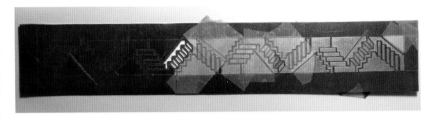

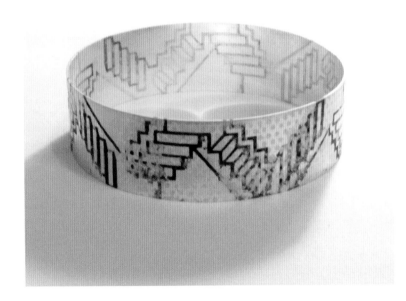

김신령 (金信姈) KIM Shin-Lyoung.
6 Types of Stairs. Bracelet. 2011.
Marriage of metals (*jeoul ipsa*),
oxidation. Fine silver, sterling silver,
nickel silver. 0.7" × 2.7" × 2.7".

김신령 (金信姈) KIM Shin-Lyoung.
Horizontal Stair. Bracelet. 2011.
Marriage of metals (*jeoul ipsa*),
oxidation. Fine and sterling silver,
nickel silver. 0.8" × 2.5" × 2.5".

김신령 (金信姈) KIM Shin-Lyoung.
Upside Down. Bracelet. 2012.
Marriage of metals (*jeoul ipsa*),
oxidation. Fine and sterling silver,
nickel silver. 0.8" × 2.5" × 2.5".

김신령 (金信姈) KIM Shin-
Lyoung. *115°–25*. Brooch. 2011.
Marriage of metals (*jeoul ipsa*),
oxidation. Fine and sterling silver,
nickel silver. 3.3" × 4.7" × 1.5".

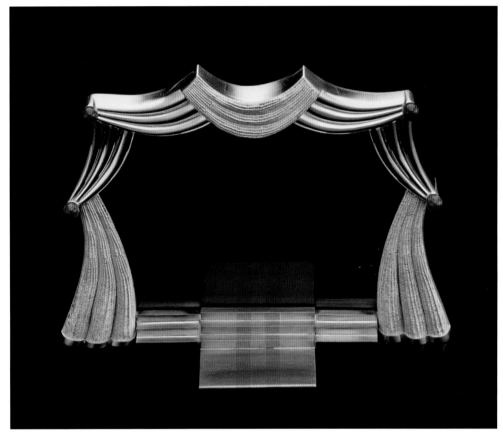

홍경희 (洪景姬) HONG Kyung Hee. *Expression III.* Brooch/pendant. 1983. Piercing, constructing, marriage of metals (*jeoul ipsa*). Sterling silver, 18K gold, copper, amethyst. 1.56" × 3.2" × 0.36". This brooch represents a traditional Korean women's top (*jeogori*) with multiple colors that represent the colorful patchwork strips of the sleeves (*saekdong*) with the technique *jeoul ipsa*.

홍경희 (洪京姬) HONG Kyung Hee. *Beautiful Memory.* Wedding symbol. 1988. Weaving, marriage of metals (*jeoul ipsa*), mitering, fabricating, riveting, setting finish. 24K gold, sterling silver, brass, copper, coral. 6.7" × 8.9" × 3.5".

CHAPTER 3

Surface-Fusing Techniques

Granulation (*Nugeum*)

Granulation was a very important technique during the Silla dynasty (fifth to sixth centuries).

This technique was probably introduced to Korea from China through the Silk Road and is thought to have originated in Sumeria 5,000 years ago. The technique was practiced mainly by Etruscans (in what is present-day Italy). One can see the subtle use of granulation in Indian and Indonesian works through museums.

Koreans were introduced to this technique during the Silla dynasty and used it to produce the king's ornaments, such as large ear ornaments, by using geometrical patterns of arabesque designs. During the Joseon dynasty, there were colorful royal hair ornaments that used filigree works covering jade carvings with enameling, kingfisher feather (*paran-bichimo*) settings and fluttering wirework at the end of small pearl, amber, or jade beads to emphasize the dancing wirework whenever the wearer moved.

According to my research, there are two different granulation techniques: (a) one using a very minute amount of solder mixed with flux as done by KIM Jinbae and (b) the original granulating technique of using fusion without solder as done by KIM Youngchang. The traditional craftspeople in Korea mainly take orders from the Buddhist monks to create special ornaments for their rituals and to make replicas for the museums as done by the above two craftsmen.

Among contemporary artists, however, this technique is used sparingly on works—not as densely as the traditional replicas shown in KIM Young-ok's work, but CHO Namu uses this fusion technique on large sections of his work with very thin 24K gold sheets.

Shin Kwon Hee uses this granulation fusion technique with phosphorus copper alloys with altering forms and designs using new physicochemical *indong* wire-fusion granulation technique. *Indong* wire is made with copper and pewter (Cu, Sn, P) with 3 alloy (C5102): Sn5%+SP0.03-0.035% +Cu+Sn+P-99.5%. It is called *Indong* granulation technique.

MIN Bokgi's way of reinterpreting traditional techniques with contemporary approaches ranges from altering forms and designs to using new physico-chemical methods. Traditional granulation is based on creating the smallest possible metal elements and attaching them to another metal surface via a thermo-chemical process. Contemporary techniques and technologies now deal with even smaller units measured in microns, the average diameter of a bacterial cell. He is interested in using these new methods to reinterpret and expand the possibilities of granulation in rapid prototyping electroforming.

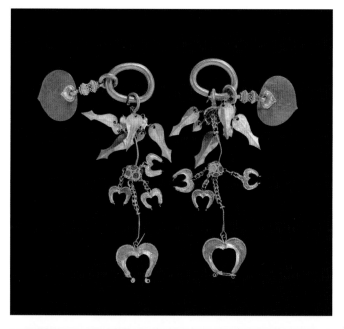

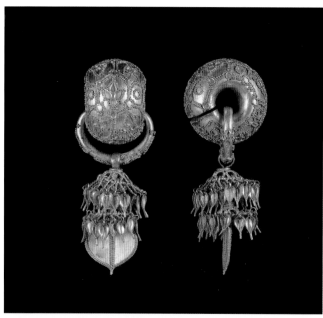

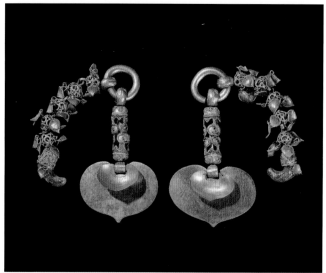

Close-up sectional view of gold earrings. Silla dynasty, early fifth century. Gold and glass. 4". *National Museum of Korea*

*Gold Earrings; Hollow Thick Ring*s. NT No. 90. Sixth century. Granulation techniques (*nugeum*). 3.5". *National Museum of Korea*

King's Gold Earrings. NT No. 156. Sixth century. 3.3". *Gongju National Museum*

Queen's Gold Earrings. NT No. 157. Sixth century. Gold and jade. 4.6". *Gongju National Museum*

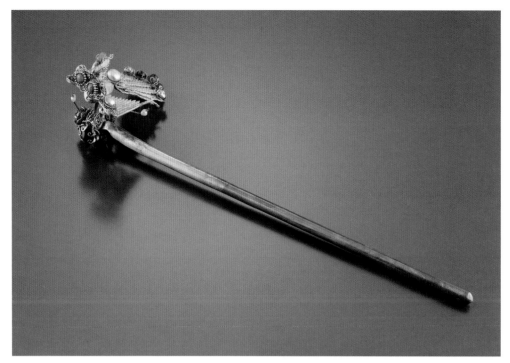

Phoenix Hair Pin Ornament. No. 123. Early twentieth century. Gold plated silver, red and blue glass stones (*hongparii* and *chongparii*), pearl, and kingfisher feather (*bichimo*). 7.9". *National Palace Museum of Korea*

Phoenix Hair Pin Ornament. No. 123 (close-up).

Bat-Shaped Perfume Pouch Norigae. No. 147. Early twentieth century. Silver with gold wire, *bichimo* (kingfisher feathers), cotton, silk thread. 16.7" × 2.6" × 2.5". *National Palace Museum of Korea*

Phoenix Ornament Hair-Stick (Binyeo). No. 124. Early twentieth century. Gold-plated silver, pearl, glass stones (*hongparii* and *chongparii*). 8.3". *National Palace Museum of Korea*

Phoenix Ornament Hair-Stick (Binyeo). No. 124 (close-up).

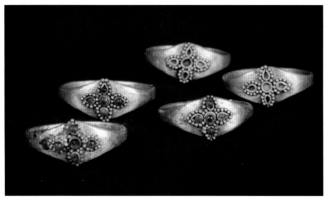

Phoenix Frontal Hair Pin. No. 135.
Early twentieth century. Wire
filigree. 3.5". *National Palace
Museum of Korea*

Gold Rings. Gold and glass. Early
fifth century. 0.7"–0.9". *Gyeongju
National Museum*

Gold Ear Ornament. No. 106. Sixth
century. *Gitak.* Granulation. 24K
gold. 2.8". *Gyeongju National
Museum*

Dogeum Nisa Pyeonbok Samjak Norigae. No. 338. Three pendants with gilded-silver wire filigree of bat designs. Seventeenth century. Used in the royal court. Gilded silver, coral, and kingfisher feather setting. 11.4". *Seokjuseon Dankook University Museum*

KIM Youngchang

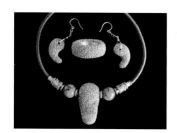

김영창 (金永昌) KIM Youngchang, Granulation (*Nugeum*) Master Craftsperson. *Summer*. Pendant and earrings. 2012. Granulation (*nugeum*). 24K gold, turquoise, wire. 1.2" × 1.2" × 1.2"; 18".

김영창 (金永昌) KIM Youngchang, Granulation (*Nugeum*) Master Craftsperson. *Gamun Buddhist Temple Priest*. Sarari reliquary container. 2007. 24K gold, pearl, crystal. 3" × 2" × 2".

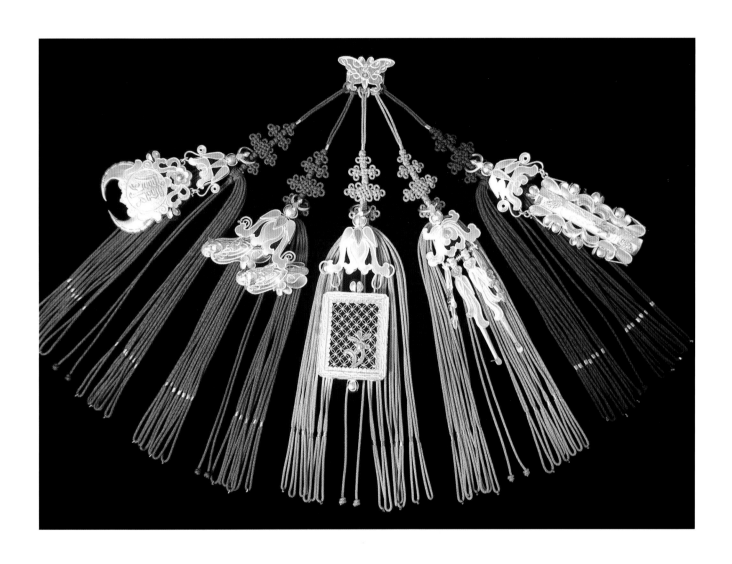

김영창 (金永昌) KIM
Youngchang, Granulation (*Nugeum*)
Master Craftsperson. *Five Parts
Norigae*. Pendant. 2010. Formed,
granulation, and filigree construction; assemble finished. Fine silver,
24K gold, silk thread Korean
macramé. 13.2" × 10" × 1".

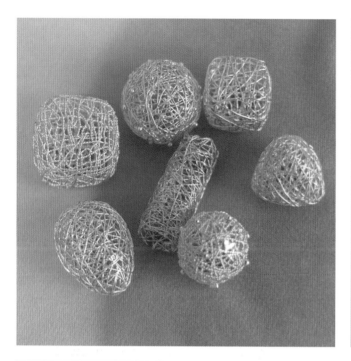

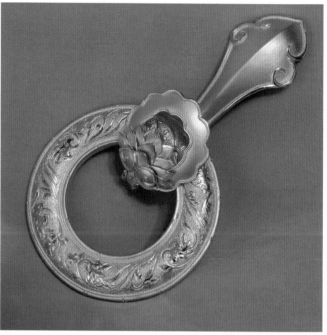

김영창 (金永昌) KIM Youngchang, Granulation (*Nugeum*) Master Craftsperson. *Replica of Silla Dynasty Beads*. Pendant beads. 2009. Granulation and filigree. 1" × 1" × 1" each.

김영창 (金永昌) KIM Youngchang, Granulation (*Nugeum*) Master Craftsperson. *Pendant for Buddhist Priest*. Pendant. 2009. Granulation and filigree. 24K gold. 2.9" × 2.9" × 0.5".

김영창 (金永昌) KIM Youngchang, Granulation (*Nugeum*) Master Craftsperson. *Circular Pendant*. Pendant. 2009. Granulation and filigree (*nugeum*). 24K gold and wire. 2.9" × 2.9" × 0.5".

김영창 (金永昌) KIM Youngchang, Granulation (*Nugeum*) Master Craftsperson. *Replica of Goguryeo King's Earring Ornament*. 2005. Forming and granulation (*nugeum*). 24K gold. 2.8" × 1.2" × 1.2".

KIM Jinbae

MASTER CRAFTSPERSON OF GRANULATION

KIM Jinbae is a full-time dedicated craftsperson and lives in the Gyeongju City Crafts Village, creating ornamental jewelry and object replicas for museums and other clients.

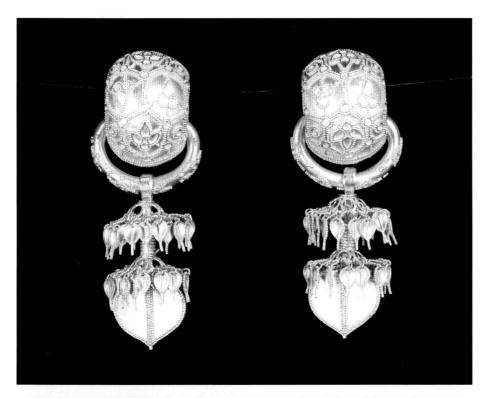

김진배 (金鎭倍) KIM Jinbae, Granulation (*Nugeum*) Master Craftsperson. *Silla King's Gold Ear Ornaments.* Earrings replica. 2012. 24K gold granulated pair of earrings. 4" × 2" × 1" each.

김진배 (金鎭倍) KIM Jinbae, Granulation (*Nugeum*) Master Craftsperson. *Silla King's Gold Ornamental Bracelet.* Ornament replica. 2014. 24K-gold-plated silver bracelet with glass. 2" × 3.5" × 3.5".

Cho's granulation processes are the new method of the traditional granulation technique. He uses the concept of granulation fusion, using a strong flame above the 24K gold sheet surface until bonding occurs. Cho employs this granulation fusion concept with 24K gold sheet to accomplish his own creative fusion. After fusing the 24K gold sheet, chasing is applied from the back for a 3-D effect. He then sets the full frontal section of the fused gold units to the damascened back unit with rivets.

조남우 (趙南宇) CHO Namu.
NB06. Bracelet. 2007. Granulation concept of fusion. 24K gold, sterling silver, diamond. 1.5" × 2.5" × 1.75".

조남우 (趙南雨) CHO Namu.
Mirage 23. Brooch and neck piece. 2006. Damascene. 24K inlaid on steel, 24K *nugeum* (fused) diamond. 1.20" × 2.3" × 0.2".

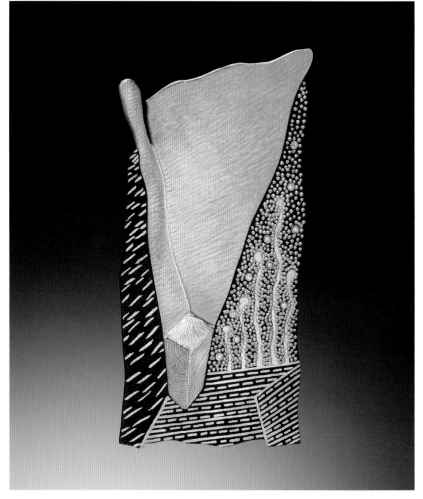

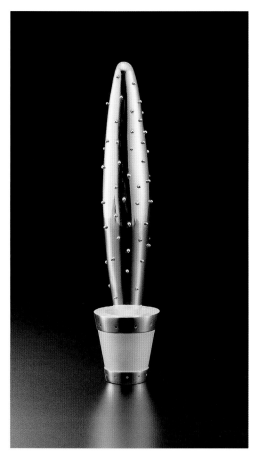

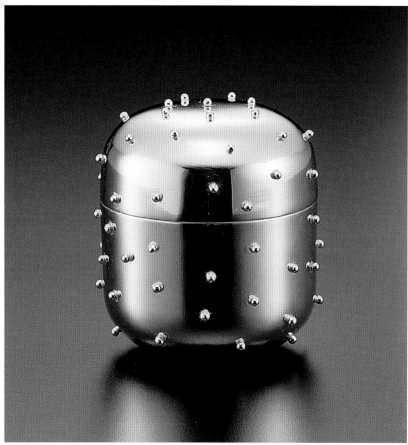

김영옥 (金榮玉) KIM Youngock.
Cactus 2002-I. Container. 2002.
Hollow forming, drilling, punching
indentations, fabricating,
fusing-granulating. Fine silver,
sterling silver. 10.4" × 2.4" × 2.4".

김영옥 (金榮玉) KIM Youngock.
Cactus 2002-VI. Container. 2002.
Hollow forming, drilling, punching
indentations, fabricating, fusing-
granulating. Fine silver, sterling
silver. 4.8" × 3.6" × 3.6".

Granulation and filigree methods originated with the Egyptians and were introduced to Korean metalcraft in the seventh century, during the Three Kingdoms period. Traditional granulation was done with 24K gold on metal surfaces.

SHIN Kwon Hee used *indong nugeum* (phosphorus copper granulation) on copper vessels using eutectic bonding granulation technique as a contemporary surface embellishment

He raised copper vessels from 1.5T (12 gauge: 2 mm) sheet metal and embellished them with intricate designs created with 14–22-gauge phosphorus copper wire specially ordered from an industrial supplier.

For this technique of eutectic bonding, an oxygen-propane or oxygen-acetylene torch is required, with a sharp-pointed torch tip. Uncut *indong* roll of wire is fused to the surface of the vessel as the torch flame moves along the wire, achieving a surface bonding or fusion without solder or flux.

Phosphorus copper (*indong*) is an alloy of copper and pewter (tin, copper, phosphorus). The alloy is composed of copper with 5 percent tin and 0.03–0.035 percent of phosphorus. It has strength, flexibility, and high heat conduction. It is easy to fuse with the correct temperature, torch flame, and distance between the object and the plate. It is also easy to plate and resistant to etching. This method is used in industry for electrical items.

신권희 (申權熙) SHIN Kwon Hee. *Chu-Nyeo.* Vessel. 1989. Phosphorus wire fusion (wire *nugeum*). Copper, phosphorus copper (*indong*), heat coloring. 43" × 13" × 13". *Private collection, Seoul, Korea*

신권희 (申權熙) SHIN Kwon Hee. *TongGuRii.* Vessel. 1988. Phosphorus wire fusion (wire *nugeum*). Copper, phosphorus copper (*indong*). 18" × 13" × 13". *Private collection, Seoul, Korea*

신권희 (申權熙) SHIN Kwon Hee. *A Woman Figure.* Tall vessel. 1988. Phosphorus wire fusion (wire *nugeum*). Copper, phosphorus copper (*indong*). 20" × 4" × 4". *Private collection, Seoul, Korea*

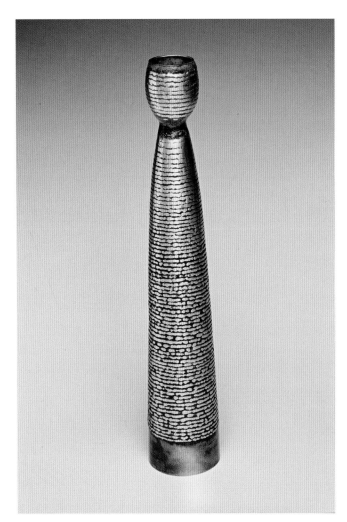

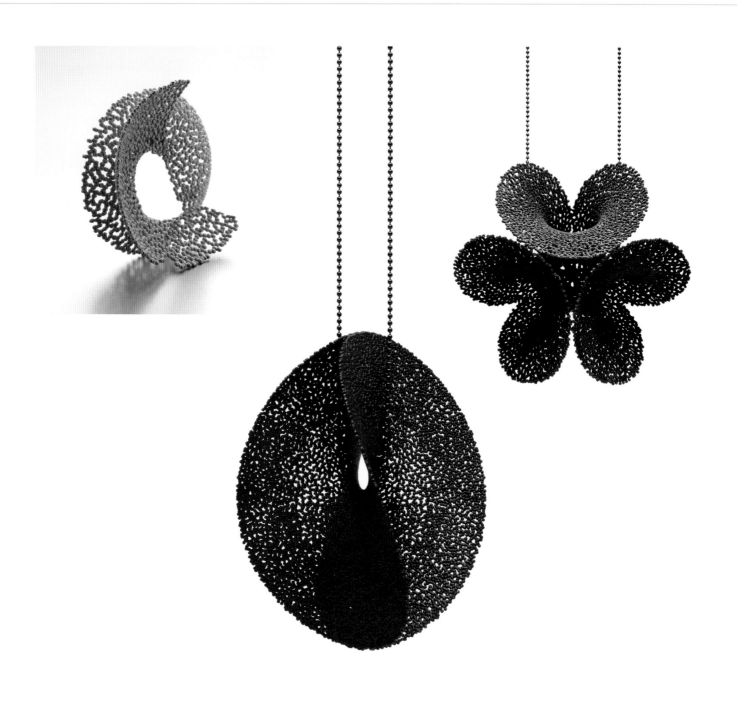

민복기 (閔復基) MIN Bogki. *From Some Error 2*. Brooch. 2011. Rapid prototyping. Gold-plated aluminum. 1" × 2.5" × 2.5".

민복기 (閔復基) MIN Bogki. *Lightecho11*. Brooch. 2014. Rapid prototyping and electroforming. Rhodium-plated aluminum. 4.9" × 3.1" × 3.1".

민복기 (閔復基) MIN Bogki. *Lightecho15*. Brooch. 2014. Rapid prototyping. Rhodium-plated aluminum. 2.8" × 3.1" × 2.3".

24K Gold Overlay (*Keum-boo*)

Keum-boo (also referred to as *kum-bu* or the official Korean romanization *geumbu*) is a Korean appliqué technique in which heat application is used to fuse 24K gold foil (0.03–0.25 mm thick) onto the surface of finished silver ornaments or objects. 24K gold guiding is only used with 0.1 micron, while *keum-boo* application is used with 24K gold foil over 100 micron (0.1 mm) and is usually used over 250 to 300 microns (0.25 to 0.3 mm)

The technique was unfamiliar in the United States and almost unheard of in its commercial industry until the late 1980s. However, *keum-boo* is a popular technique in Korea that has been detected as early as the *Goryeo* dynasty in the twelfth century on acupuncture needle cases, as well as inside the bowl of silver spoons from the *Joseon* dynasty and the tips of the chopsticks among the royal court. Contemporary usage of *keum-boo* is applied to finished silver objects such as 2-D or 3-D jewelry, holloware, and tea and coffee sets, and is especially popular on flatware and utensils.

There is an East Asian belief that the ingestion of pure gold will improve health and well-being. Many herbal medicines are covered with very thin sheets of pure gold. Similarly, acupuncture needles are often made of high-karat gold, in the belief that the effectiveness of the treatment will be enhanced. Many Korean silver utensils are decorated with 24K gold overlay in the form of letters and patterns that convey wishes for good health, wealth, and longevity. In most cases the ornament is set in the interior of a cup or bowl, or within the bowl of a spoon, to ensure that food will contact the gold and therefore assimilate its positive characteristics before being consumed.

Keum-boo is accomplished by heating silver to bond gold foil with applied pressure from a burnisher, a metal tool for ironing metal surfaces. The technique is applied either on a smooth or a textured surface. The object is heated to bring up a thin layer of fine silver to the surface. The 24K gold foil is applied with heat (around 700°F) and pressure to produce a permanent bond.

24K Gold Overlay (*Keum-boo*) Process
by Komelia Hongja Okim

Supply List:
24K gold foil (0.025–0.03 mm)
Curved-tip tweezers
#01 fine brush
Sharp pair of surgical scissors
X-Acto knife with a few different sharp blades
Tracing paper
Baking soda
Soft cloths and extrasoft toothbrush
Cup (non-plastic) for water to quench hot metal-burnishing tools
Thick and tight-fitting cotton gloves to protect the artist from heat while working on the hotplate or torch
Kitchen scrubbing pad
Liquid dish soap
Ammonia
Tripods
Portable torches
Hot-acid pickle bath
Tumbler with stainless-steel shots
Teaspoon to carry bonding agent
CMC (available from ceramic suppliers) or gum tragacanth powder mixed with water
Fine brass brush

Step 1:
Before starting *keum-boo* application, one must get rid of all fire scale, which is a layer of oxides that appears on silver alloys, forming a red-purple discoloration.

To remove fire scale, heat the work with a soft flame after the final polishing. Heat at about 700°F until a black scale shows on the surface. Let the piece cool a second before immersing into the hot pickle (acid) solution and leave until the surface color is a frosty silver-white tone.

Clean by using a fine-brass or nickel wire brush and soapy water, or use a soft toothbrush or cloths. Rinse under running faucet water. This process is repeated until no more black-colored fire scale appears when the piece is heated. It may take one to three repetitions before the piece is ready for *keum-boo* application. Do not use a wire brush on the piece after the final application.

Step 2:
Cool the object completely before *keum-boo* application. Apply *keum-boo* on the desired places with saliva or a weak solution of CMC, gum arabic, or gum tragacanth powder mixed with water (not commercially premixed solution). Let the *keum-boo* dry before next step.

Step 3:
Place the object on a hot plate (do not preheat) or soft torch flame, heating gradually (to about 700°F) until the wet spit or gum solution subsides. Check bonding by using the side of a burnishing tool pressed lightly left to right. For bigger objects, it is ideal to use both a hot plate and portable torch.

If bonding is starting, turn off the torch (but leave the object on the hot plate) and burnish over entire design from outer corners to center until the *keum-boo* gold foil design is fully bonded.

Wear cotton gloves to handle the metal burnisher and torch flame. Cool the object for 5–10 minutes, then pickle in very clean, hot pickling solution. For large objects, use two hotplates and a portable acetylene torch above the large metal screen, good enough to bring the object to the right temperature for applying *keum-boo*. When using only the torch, heat the object away from the *keum-boo* patterns, and when the right temperature is reached (sizzling stops and the black color disappears around the *keum-boo* shapes), put away the torch flame and start burnishing for good bonding.

Step 4:
Final finishing is accomplished by going over the surface lightly with a fine scrubbing kitchen pad to get rid of burnishing marks. If desired, you may oxidize the entire object or paint around the *keum-boo* shapes with liver of sulfur. Remove excess oxidation with a scrubber or polish the object carefully outside *keum-boo* areas.

Step 5:
After oxidizing the surface, finish with desired highlighting gradation, set stones and pin backs, and do the final polish in the steel shot tumbler for 5 minutes for the final polished appearance (optional). You can apply Renaissance wax or museum wax to buff the surface with fine cloths for protection.

Process for *The Revelation:* *"The Humanbeing Blue"*

1. Form the human figures out of silver and place on *keum-boo* gold foil
2. Trace the outline of the figures firmly. Cut out with scissors.
3. Place the gold foil on the figures. Heat underneath.
4. Fix the gold foil by pressing and rubbing with a burnisher.
5. Add scratches with a pointed tool to express the passing of time.
6. Pickle and oxidize with liver of sulfur.

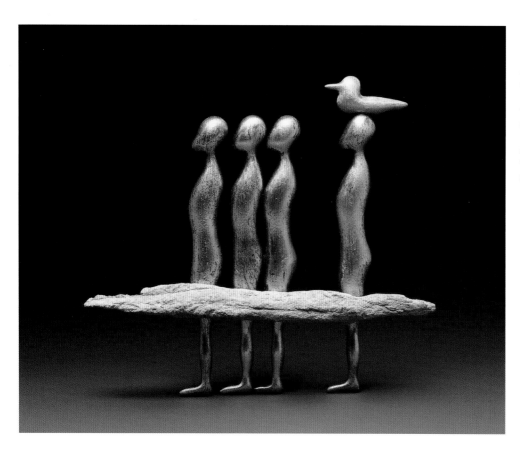

김정후 (金娗厚) KIM Jung-Hoo. *The Revelation: "The Humanbeing Blue."* Brooch. 1991. *Keum-boo.* Sterling silver, fossilized ivory, 24K gold. 3¾" × 4¾" × ¾".

I have been thinking about what the nature of us is through the contrast of the fixed gaze, which looking back at the past and simultaneously looking forward to the future makes another world of space-time.

Process for *The Rain:*

1. Put the human figures (which are made of silver) on the *keum-boo* gold foil.
2. Firmly trace the outline of the human figures.
3. Cut the *keum-boo* foil bigger than the original line in order to cover the figures completely.
4. Place this *keum-boo* gold foil on the human figures.
5. Place heat underneath the silver human figures.
6. Fix the gold foil by pressing and rubbing with a burnisher.

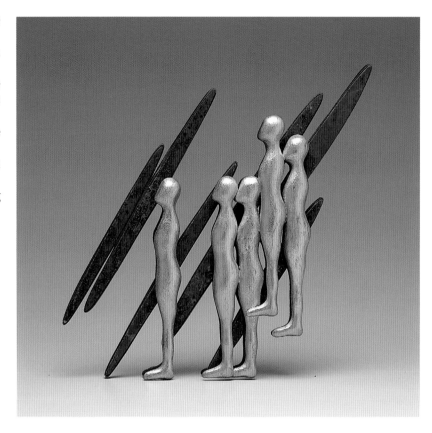

김정후 (金姃厚) KIM Jung-Hoo.
The Rain. Brooch. 2009. *Keum-boo.*
Sterling silver, lapis lazuli, 24K gold.
3⅛" × 2⅝" × ½".

Each life is directed by what each person thinks is the most important. At every moment when I should decide, I ask myself what I think is important. Through *The Rain* brooch I want to try thinking carefully about what is the most important to human life, such as water (rain) being essential to human health.

김정후 (金姃厚) KIM Jung-Hoo.
The Chair. Brooch. 1997.
Keum-boo. Sterling silver, slate,
24K gold. 2⅝" × 3⅝ × ¾".

The featureless human figure with the chair on the ox game background (a popular children's game similar to hopscotch) allows the viewer to imagine or contemplate a scene of her or his own making.

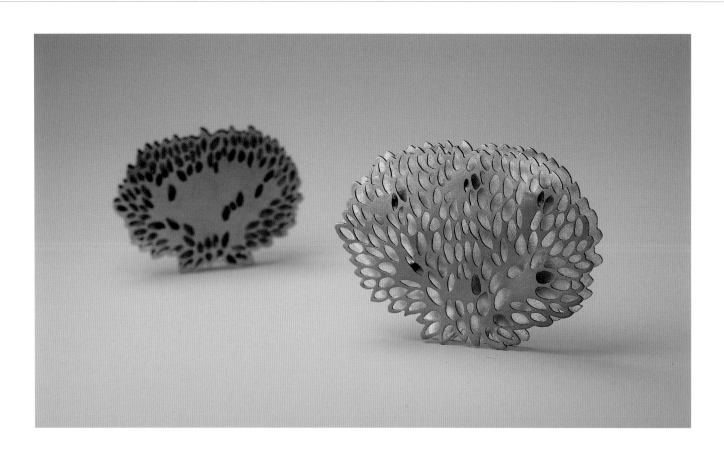

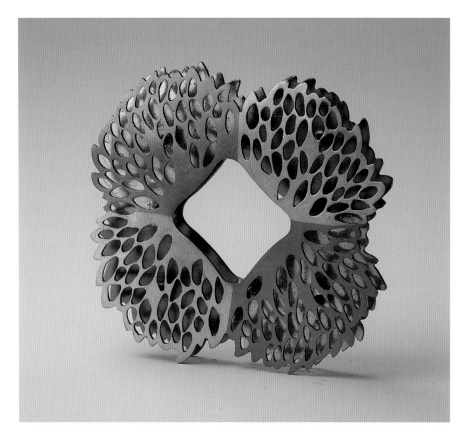

김경희 (金璟禧) KIM Kyung Hee.
Their Own Story 1. Brooches. 2007.
Piercing, constructing, oxidizing,
fusing with 24K gold overlay
(*keum-boo*). Sterling silver, 24K
gold. 1.7" × 2.3" × 0.4" each.

김경희 (金璟禧) KIM Kyung Hee.
Their Own Story 2. Brooch. 2007.
Piercing, constructing, oxidizing,
fusing with 24K gold overlay
(*keum-boo*). Sterling silver, 24K
gold. 2.7" × 2.8" × 0.4".

김승희 (金昇姬) KIM Seung Hee. *Cubic*. Earrings and neck piece. 2004. *Keum-boo*. Sterling silver, 24K gold. 22"; 1.2" each.

김승희 (金昇姬) KIM Seung Hee. Faces of *ARMAN I, II, III*. 3 brooches. 2000. Sterling silver, 24K gold (*keum-boo*). 2.4" × 2.4" × 0.5" each.

김승희 (金昇姬) KIM Seung Hee. *Pebbles*. Two hollow-chain necklaces. 2016. Synclastic, *keum-boo* technique. Amber, turquoise, 24K gold *keum-boo*, sterling silver. 24" round each.

김성수 (金成洙) KIM Sungsoo.
*King's Dinner Casserole on
Charcoal HotPot (Shinsollo).*
Chafing dish. 2000. Raising,
forming, fabricating, riveting,
texturing, and oxidized. Iron,
sterling silver, copper, 24K gold foil
overlay fusion (*keum-boo*), wood.
28" × 34" × 34".
   Shinsollo is a traditional hot pot
of the Korean royal court, with an
iron charcoal burner underneath
the iron burner to keep food warm.

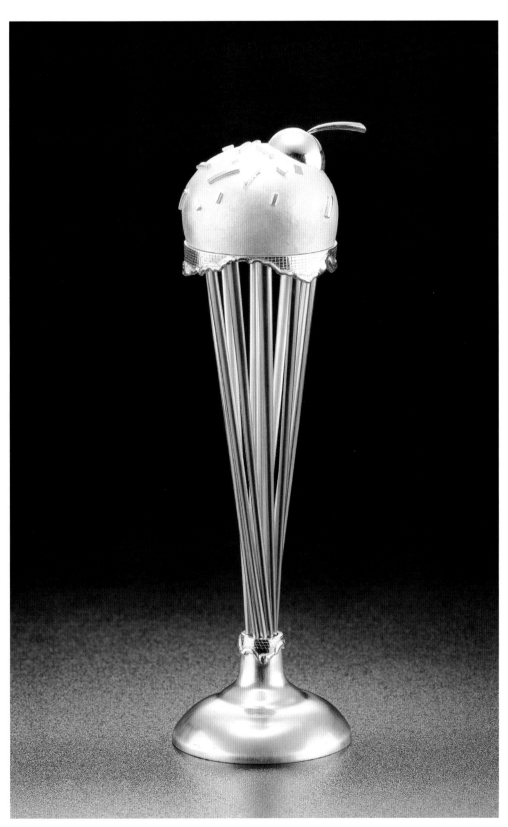

김영옥 (金榮玉) KIM Youngock. *Summer.* Chopstick-holding cone. 2000. *Keum-boo.* Fine and sterling silver, 24K gold. 10.8″ × 4.8″ × 4.8″.

Summer was created using a combination of roll-printing, raising, forming, constructing, and *keum-boo* (surface embellishment) technique. The top shape functions as a lid, with the base as a sculptural object. The chocolate chip shapes and the chopsticks are embellished with *keum-boo* technique to signify the preciousness of the eating utensils.

KOH Heeseung

고희승 (高嬉丞) KOH Heeseung. *Evoking Traces*. Ring with object. 2014. Forming, fabricating, enameling, and fusing 24K gold overlay (*keum-boo*) on silver. Enameling and *keum-boo*. 24K gold, porcelain, copper, enameling. 3.54" × 1.96" × 1.18" each.

My work aims to intensify the internal and essential characteristics of materials rather than external beauty of objects. I intend to make a simple and primitive shape by using natural and vintage texture without decoration.

LEE Hyewon

이혜원 (李惠園) LEE Hyewon. *Circle*. 2000. Wine bottle and cups. Raising, forming, constructing, 24K gold overlaying (*keum-boo*). Silver, 24K gold. 7.6" × 4" × 4"; 1.8" × 2.8" × 2.8".

이혜원 (李惠園) LEE Hyewon. *Square*. Brooch. 2013. Raising, forming, constructing, 24K gold overlaying (*keum-boo*). Silver, 24K gold. 1.8" × 2.2" × 0.4"; 1" × 3.2" × 0.4".

I weave a story based on the basic rules of a solid body, variations of geometrical forms, effects of light and shadow, and the relationship between an object and its surroundings, all of which are the language of my art.

LEE Hyung Kyu

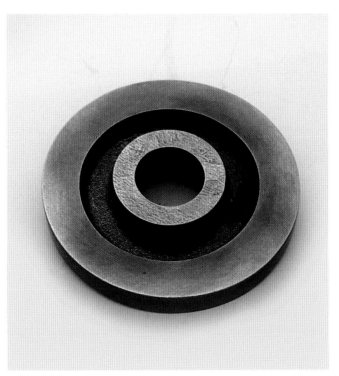

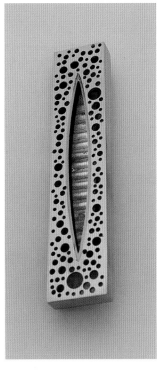

이형규 (李炯奎) LEE Hyung Kyu. *Circle 1007*. Brooch. 2010. Roll printing, fabricating, oxidizing and fusing, *keum-boo*. Sterling silver, 24K gold. 2" × 2" × 0.3".

이형규 (李炯奎) LEE Hyung Kyu. *Inner Space*. Brooch. 2011. Roll printing, marriage of metals (*jeoul ipsa*), fabricating, oxidizing and fusing, *keum-boo*. Sterling silver, 24K gold, copper. 2.7" × 0.7" × 0.3".
   This work is about the space in the brooch and its faithful relationship to the internal psychological space. The restrained rectangular form symbolizes perfection and logic. The red copper color of the boundary is connected with the inner space. Both the *keum-boo* applied in the center and the silver color covering the material of the brooch indicate the great significance of creating harmony.

LONG, Janet

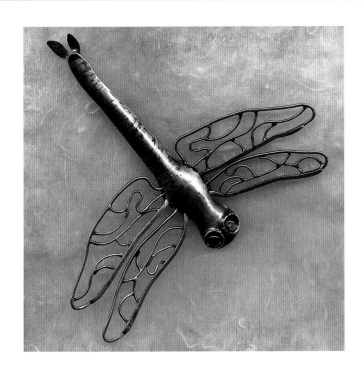

LONG, Janet. *Dragon Fly*. Brooch. 2008. Hydraulic press, construction, 24K gold foil *keum-boo* overlay, oxidation. Sterling silver, 24K gold, emerald. 2.75 " × 2.75" × 0.75".
   Silver wire forms the delicate and lacy cell structure of the wings. The striped pattern of the dragonfly's body was produced with *keum-boo* technique.

오병옥 (吳秉旭) OH Byungwuk. *Brooch 11-1.* Brooch. 2011. Casting, constructing, fusing 24K gold overlay (*keum-boo*). Fine silver, 24K gold. 1.6" × 1.6" × 0.4" each.

오병옥 (吳秉旭) OH Byungwuk. *Necklace 11-1.* Necklace. 2011. *Keum-boo.* Fine silver, 24K gold. 8" × 8" × 1".

Necklace 11-1 is reminiscent of rocks worn smooth from many years of wind and water erosion. These are between man-made forms and forms found in nature. This work has a quiet sense of beauty.

김홍자 (金弘子) OKIM Komelia Hongja. *Niobium-scape*. Neck piece. 1996. Anodized, constructed, assembled, and oxidized to highlight. Sterling silver, 24K gold *keum-boo*, niobium. 16" × 18" × 0.5". *Private collection, Baltimore, Maryland*

김홍자 (金弘子) OKIM Komelia Hongja. *The Blue Q Landscape*. Q-tip box. 1987. Anodizing titanium, mitering, assemble setting, fabricating, 24K *keum-boo* overlaying and finishing. Sterling silver, titanium, 24K gold *keum-boo*. 8" × 6" × 6". *Private collection, Seoul, Korea*

Reflecting the city scenes, this functional Q-tip box utilizes contemporary anodizing technique with the Korean traditional technique of *keum-boo*.

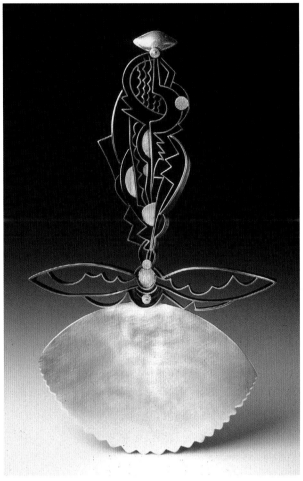

김홍자 (金弘子) OKIM Komelia
Hongja. *The Perfect Harmony*. Coffee
pot / teapot. 1996. Raising, forming,
assembling, curling wires,
fabricating, 24K *keum-boo*
overlaying, Korean traditional
nineteenth-century technique, and
oxidizing to highlight. Fine and
sterling silver, 24K gold *keum-boo*.
10" × 9.5" × 5"; 5.6" × 5.5" × 3".
Collection of LA Teapot Museum

김홍자 (金弘子) OKIM Komelia
Hongja. *Mountainscape*. Cake server.
1999. Forming, mitering, hydraulic
forming, fabricating, applying Korean
techniques of 24K gold foil
keum-boo overlaying and 24K gold
leaf *keumpak* application and
oxidation. Sterling silver, 24K gold
foil and leaf. 12" × 10" × 1".
*Collection of Victoria & Albert
Museum, London*

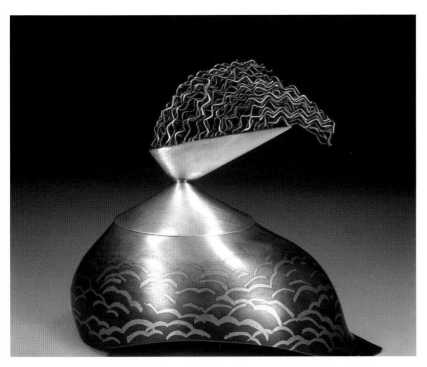

김홍자 (金弘子) OKIM Komelia Hongja. *By the Seaside #3.* Vessel. 1996. A woman longing for seaside landscape. Forming, raising, fabricating, 24K gold *keum-boo* overlay, and oxidized. Fine and sterling silver and 24K gold *keum-boo.* 7.5" × 7" × 5". *Collection of Museum of Arts & Design, New York City*

김홍자 (金弘子) OKIM Komelia Hongja. *Autumn Contemplation.* Vessel. 1999. Raising, forming, assembling, curling wires, fabricating, 24K *keum-boo* overlaying, and oxidizing to highlight. Fine and sterling silver and 24K gold *keum-boo.* 7.5" × 10" × 5". *Collection of Yunnan Hanrongxuan Culture & Art Museum, Kookmin City, China*

As a Korean American metal artist, I used *keum-boo* techniques learned from Professor Okim in my Morning Dew and other series. These highlight my heritage as well as the essence of sparkling morning dew. The shape of morning dew inspires me as I face each new day and realize the wonderful new beginning phenomenon of the sunrise. Using the *keum-boo* method, I employ gold drops to represent the shape of the dew, which beautifully glistens, reflecting my homeland and my memories.

김정화 (金晶華) PAIK, KIM Junghwa. *Infinity I*. Brooch. 2017. Forming, oxidizing, fusing *keum-boo*. Silver, 24K gold. 5" × 3" × 3".

김정화 (金晶華) PAIK, KIM Junghwa. *Blossoming*. Brooch. 2013. Texturing, forming, fabricating, oxidizing, *keum-boo*. Silver, 24K gold. 3" × 4" × 1".

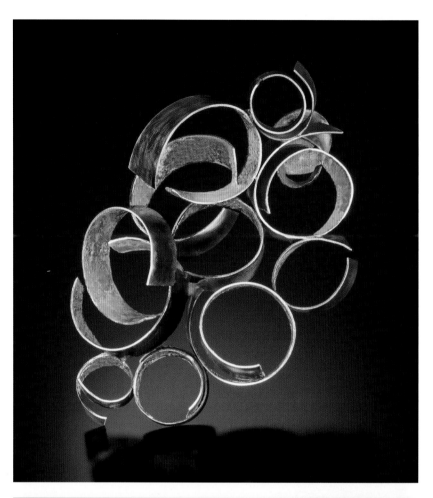

김정화 (金晶華) PAIK, KIM
Junghwa. *Infinity II*. Brooch.
2017. Forming, oxidizing, fusing
keum-boo. Silver, 24K gold.
5" × 2" × 2".

PARK Sangsook

This work embodies a narrative of my reflection on the transition from my identity as a Korean woman to a new identity living in American culture. The narratives are about my memories of the old place from a new cultural place and space. My work draws a peaceful relationship between people and personal connections. I balance myself in two cultural places in various forms. In the process of cultural-identity transition, my work is inspired by my research and knowledge of Korean traditional aesthetics in metals and culture.

박상숙 (朴相淑) PARK Sangsook. *My Family.* Brooch. 2014. Scoring, fabricating and fusing, *keum-boo.* Sterling silver, 24K gold foil. 3" × 1.75" × 0.5".

VERNON, Estelle

My jewelry designs are influenced by visual and tactile experiences. Whether it's leaves on trees, the roughness of bark, or the intricacies of oriental textile design, I distill these images into elegant simplicity. My jewelry is embellished with 24K gold overlay (*keum-boo*) techniques, which enhance texture. I have been incorporating this Korean *keum-boo* technique in my work for the past thirty years, since studying with Professor Komelia Okim at Montgomery College in Rockville, Maryland.

VERNON, Estelle. *Bryce Series Leaf Pendant 1.* Pendant. 2013. Roll printed, die formed, fabricated, and oxidized. Sterling silver, 24K gold, stainless-steel and gold-plated wire neck. 2" × 0.75" × 0.25"; 18" neck wire. *Photo, Victor Wolansky*

VERNON, Estelle. Yellowstone Series 2: *Square Pendant 1.* Pendant. 2013. Roll printed and oxidized. Sterling silver, 24K gold, stainless-steel and gold-plated neck wire. 1.38" × 1.18" × 1.25"; 18" neck wire. *Photo, Victor Wolansky*

I learned Korean *keum-boo* overlay and other techniques during the summer workshops I hosted at Tainan National University for the Arts, in Taiwan, for my students in 1999 and 2011, taught by Professor Komelia Okim. I used gold application with various sizes of geometric shapes within the round circles, as seen in the old Chinese metal coins, and found it quite exciting to combine two shapes as in a dual concept joining Korean and Chinese cultures, the same as old and new coins melding in my containers. These shapes symbolize good luck and signify both old Chinese coins and melding dual concepts of combining Korean and Chinese cultures in harmony, such as in these vessels of the container and the tea/coffee.

王梅珍 WANG Mei-Jen. *Vessel*. Container with lid. 2003. Raising, forming, constructing, *keum-boo* overlay, high polished and pickled in acid bath for frosted white color. Sterling silver, 24K gold. 7.9" × 5.9" × 5.9".

王梅珍 WANG Mei-Jen. *Teapot*. Container with lid and handle. 2004. Raising, forming, constructing, *keum-boo* overlay, high polished and pickled in acid bath for frosted white color. Sterling silver, 24K gold, drift-wood carved. 8.3" × 8.2" × 5.1".

Won Misun was inspired by the Korean traditional patchwork wrapping cloth *jogakbo* and scientific interpretation of fractal-geometry theory. She wants to associate the beauty of rhythmical structure from *jogakbo* with her jewelry, using a "patchwork" of circles and ovals.

Because the composition of *jogakbo* is based on nature, she employs fractal geometry in order to analyze the complex compositions of *jogakbo*. She makes a variety of structures and patterns from one sheet of silver, creating playful forms on their own or in combination with other materials. She also applies the ancient Korean technique of *keum-boo* (24K gold foil overlay) to her jewelry to maximize the complexity of patterns and structures.

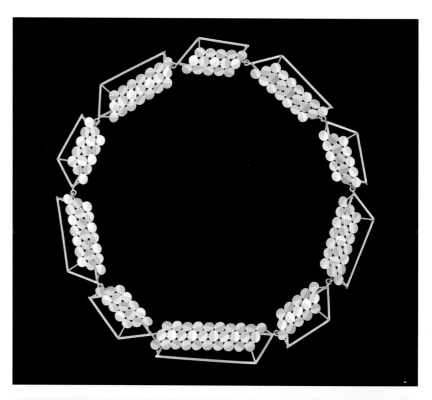

원미선 (元美善) WON Misun. *3D Rhombus*. Necklace. 2017. Hand piercing, bending, fabricating, fusing *keum-boo*, and burnishing. Sterling silver, *keum-boo* (24K gold). 8.0" × 8.0" × 0.6".

원미선 (元美善) WON Misun. *Parallelogram*. Rings. 2017. Hand piercing, bending, fabricating, fusing *keum-boo*, and burnishing. Sterling silver, *keum-boo* (24K gold), 18K yellow gold, garnet, tourmaline. 0.9" × 0.5" × 1.1" each.

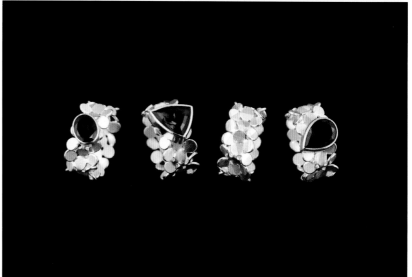

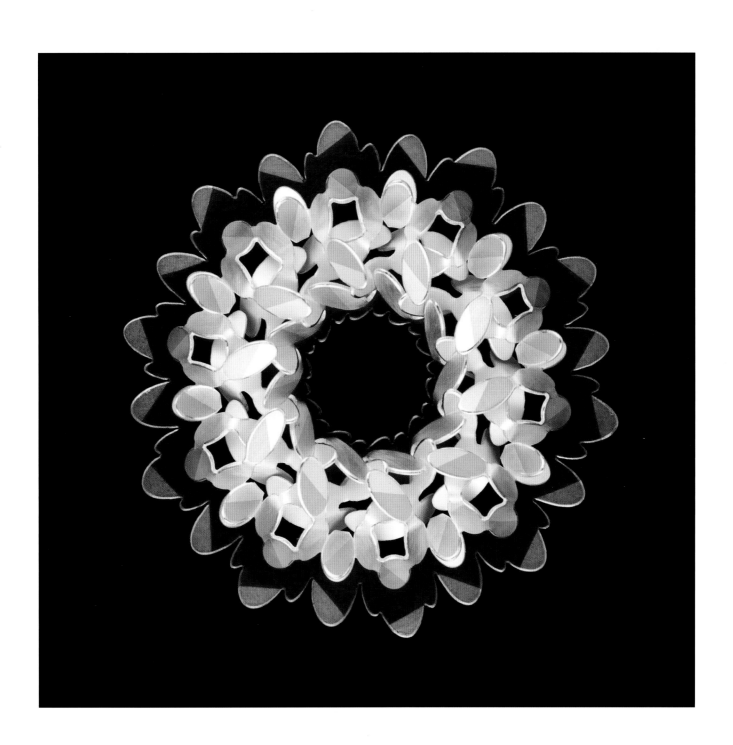

원미선 (元美善) WON Misun.
Circular Ovals I. Brooch. 2015.
Hand piercing, bending, fabricating, fusing *keum-boo*, oxidizing,
burnishing, and riveting. Sterling
silver, *keum-boo* (24K gold).
2.5" × 2.5" × 0.6".

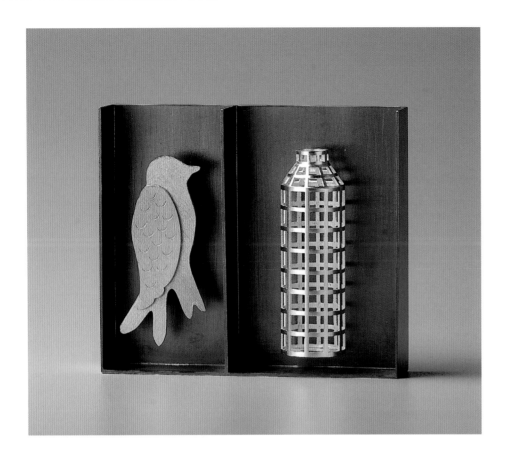

우진순 (禹眞純) WOO Jinsoon.
Bird & Vase. Brooch. 2013.
Keum-boo. Sterling silver, 24K
gold. 2.3" × 2.7" × 0.4".

In *Bird & Vase*, a bird silhouette
and a flower vase speak to
elements of hidden beauty in the
natural world.

우진순 (禹眞純) WOO Jinsoon.
Memory. Brooch. 2013. *Keum-boo*. Sterling silver, 24K gold.
2" × 2.8" × 0.4".

The artist was inspired by
photographs depicting bright objects
on dark backgrounds. Each piece
shown here is divided into two sides:
one side features the silhouette of a
natural form of *keum-boo*, while the
other side is a highly polished silver
structure in relief.

In *Memory*, the juxtaposition of
the human face and the tower
creates a dialogue, referencing
architectural space.

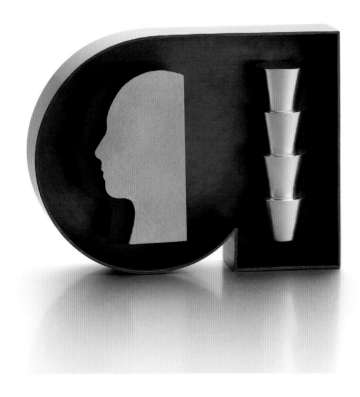

Overall patterns and textures have always fascinated me and been an integral part of my work. Having long admired the rich variety of surface embellishments in Korean metalsmithing, in particular *poamok saang-gum* (Korean-style damascene) and *keum-boo*, I was delighted to meet highly regarded Korean metalsmith Komelia Okim while she was a visiting professor at the University of Wisconsin–Madison. In 1986, Professor Okim visited my metals program at the University of Wisconsin–Whitewater and gave an exciting workshop and demonstration of traditional Korean techniques.

These brooches were executed by first fusing 24K gold sheet to fine-silver sheet, using the *keum-boo* process of heating and burnishing. This gilded silver was embossed using a previously etched patterned brass plate in a rolling mill. The embossed sheet was formed by using mallets and wooden stakes. Alternate layers of the design were similarly embossed. Several of the layered components were enameled. Finally, the separate elements of the brooch were joined by using cold connections.

THREADGILL, Linda. *Rosette Brooch 117-E.* 2017. *Keum-boo*, etching, enameling, patina. Fine and sterling silver, 24K gold foil, enamel. 3" × 3" × 0.5". *Photo, artist*

THREADGILL, Linda. *Rosette Brooch 217-E.* 2017. *Keum-boo*, etching, enameling. Fine and sterling silver, 24K gold foil, enamel. 3" × 3" × 0.5". *Photo, artist*

THREADGILL, Linda. *Rosette Brooch 317-E.* 2017. *Keum-boo*, etching, enameling, patina. Fine and sterling silver, 24K gold, 18K gold, enamel. 3" × 3" × 0.75". *Photo, artist*

BORSETTI, Liz

BORSETTI, Liz. *Large and Small Studs.* Earrings. 2016. Casting, constructing, 24K gold overlay (*keum-boo*). Fine silver and 24K gold. 0.75" × 0.5"; 0.5" × 0.25".

CHI Youngji

지영지 (池映知) CHI Youngji. *Bubble Series 1.* Ring. 2016. *Keum-boo*, oxidation. Sterling silver, 24K gold foil. 1.2" × 1.2" × 0.8".

장윤우 (張潤宇) CHANG
Yoon-Woo. *White Flowers.* Flower
vase. Raising, constructing,
assembling, and 24K gold overlay
(*keum-boo*). Sterling silver and 24K
gold. 4.8" × 5" × 5".

HU, Sophia

I am an architect and a self-taught silver-smith. Sterling silver, gold, and other natural materials are my new building materials in these small-scale sculptures.

HU, Sophia. *Origami Butterfly*. Cuff. 2016. Punching, folding, fabricating, *keum-boo* with 23K gold overlay fusing, and finished oxidation. 2" × 2" × 1.5" (side view).

HUR Misook

허미숙 (許美淑) HUR Misook. *Yellow Birds*. Brooches. 2009. Casting, fabricating, fusing 24K gold overlay on silver (*keum-boo*). Sterling silver, 24K gold. 1.8" × 2" × 0.25" each. *Photo, artist*

HUR Misook is enamored by nature and draws inspiration from the constantly changing and ever-repeating cycle of life. This work provokes a sense of movement with a gesture to the cycles of life.

24K Gold Leaf Overlay (*Keumpak*)

Keumpak (the official Korean Romanization is *geumbak*) is a 24K gold leaf (thinner than tissue) brush-painting technique that has been used traditionally for royal writings, important Buddhist inscriptions, and parts of paintings and statues in order to express preciousness, greatness, long-lasting durability, and royal status. The 24K gold leafing (*keumpak*) is also used to wrap food and herbal medicine. The 24K gold leaf or powder is applied with a very thin layer of diluted animal or fish gelatin as glue for bonding. Korean sumac lacquering (*ottchil*) is applied over the gold leafing to protect it from discoloration and add to the richness of the gold colors.

Historically, the Korean king's ceremonial objects and joinery were covered in 24K gold leaf to preserve the ornaments' value. Kings' jade belts display carved inscriptions filled with 24K gold powder inlay. Today in Korea, as in other Asian countries, gold leaf and gold powder are applied to objects, tea, and wine to enhance health. The 24K gold printed on special clothing emphasizes important occasions.

Keum-boo application is done with heat, whereas *keumpak* uses organic glue bonding without heat application.

Contemporary Artist Technical References

CHOI Hyunchil

Choi Hyunchil is inspired to create large cast vessels for potpourri to keep rooms fresh. His themes involve family portraits depicting wife, husband, son, and daughter in an abstract form of birds. The birds' beaks usually have holes, allowing the scent to permeate the environment.

Choi first creates his objects in plaster carvings and defines them with surface patterns and finishing before making rubber molds from them. Wax molds produced from the rubber molds are then cut into two to four sections and, with centrifugal casting, cast in sterling silver in several sections. After surface finishing is finalized, sections are silver-soldered to a completed form.

Some of his finished objects are colored according to his design with car paints, and cut 24K gold leaf (*keumpak)* patterns or fine-silver leaf (*eumpak*) are carefully attached to the surfaces, using organic sizing glue (diluted cowhide glue). A final coating of highly diluted glue is applied to varnish the object.

최현칠 (崔鉉七) CHOI Hyunchil. *Potpourri Sent Container 94-2.* Object. 1994. Bronze, paint, fine-silver leaf (*eunbak*). 40" × 40" × 21".

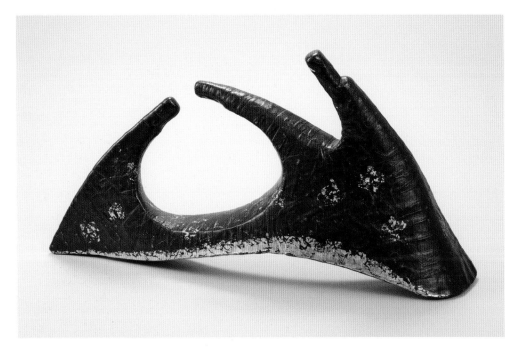

최현칠 (崔鉉七) CHOI Hyunchil. *Potpourri Scent Container 94.* Object. 1994. *Keumpak.* Bronze, paint, 24K gold leaf. 21" × 40" × 20".

최현칠 (崔鉉七) CHOI Hyunchil. *Potpourri Scent Container 95.* Object. 1995. *Keumpak.* Bronze, 24K gold leaf. 40" × 40" × 20".

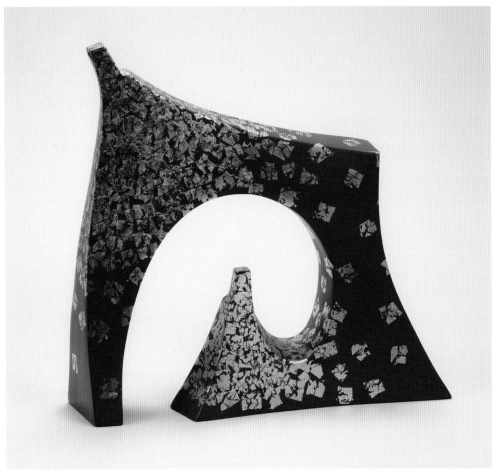

CHO Namu

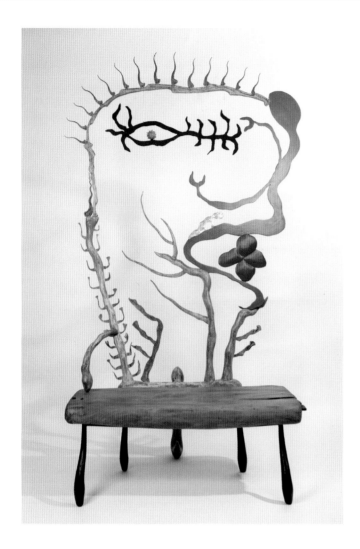

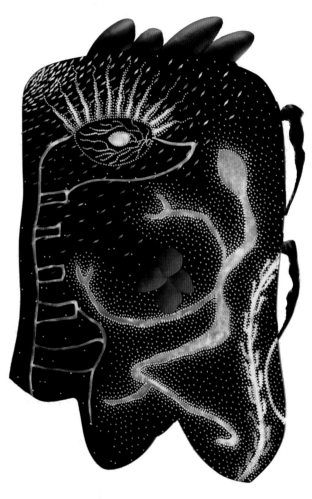

조남우 (趙南宇) CHO Namu.
Heavenly Luck 1. Bench. 2004.
Antique wood-board chair with
steel iron legs. Fabricated copper
elements, patina, colored with
acrylic paint, 24K gold leaf on
carved wood creature. Copper,
steel cast iron, 24K gold leafing,
patina, acrylic paint, wood.
82" × 49" × 25".

In *Heavenly Luck 1*, Cho uses the
image of a chair as a self-portrait,
sitting and meditating on his interior
and exterior environment.

조남우 (趙南宇) CHO Namu.
Heavenly Luck 2. Wall relief. 2005.
Fabricated copper elements,
patina, colored with acrylic paint,
24K gold leaf (*keumpak*) on rivets.
Steel, copper, acrylic paint,
threaded rivets, 24K gold leaf.
38" × 26" × 11".

In *Heavenly Luck 2*, Cho
expresses heavenly mighty power,
energy, and God's eye watching
over one's well-being and
aspirations. The images represent
a hard-working people and their
future generations (red color). They
are to be blessed with energy and
hope, symbolized by deer horn,
and remembrance beyond their
given life span, symbolized by
turtle imagery.

김홍자 (金弘子) OKIM Komelia
Hongja. *Fall Promenade*. Sculpture.
1993. Band-saw cutting, fabricating, curling wires, chemical patina,
oil painting, and 24K gold leaf
keumpak. Copper, brass, patina, oil
paint. 12" × 12" × 6". *Private
collection, Honolulu, Hawaii*

SAKIHARA, Carol. *Kailua Beach.* Bowl. Raising, chasing and repoussé (*tachul*), oxidizing, and 24K gold leafing (*keumpak*). Copper, 24K gold leaf, oxidation. 3.78" × 8.5" × 8.5" (top view).

Since I learned these techniques, I have been using this Korean method of 24K-gold-leafing work to apply to my metalwork for contrasting with the metal background and the added 24K gold colors. My inspiration for the bowl is Kailua Beach, Hawaii, where waves driven by northeasterly winds are illuminated by sunlight reflected from the Koolau Mountains.

SAKIHARA, Carol. *Kailua Beach* (side view).

CHAPTER 4

Chasing and Repoussé
(*Tachul*)

Ancient methods of creating 3-D relief and details have been especially popular in ancient Korean metal crafts. Chasing and repoussé (*tachul*) methods can be seen in many objects from the Three Kingdoms period (957 BCE–676 CE) and continue on in contemporary works.

The process begins with pitch melted and fused to a hardwood board. The melted pitch must be the proper consistency and harden enough before it can be used to hammer details into the metal.

Specialized repoussé tools and hammers are used to push metal from back to front and form details. Most details are added from the front by using sharp chasing tools on the raised forms.

This technique of using chasing and repoussé by employing pitch (or wax) and repeatedly annealing hardened metal, as well as refilling and emptying the pitch until all details are accomplished, is unchanged in contemporary chasing and repoussé.

Tall Mirror Frame. Duk5704. Goryeo dynasty, twelfth–thirteenth centuries. Gold-plated silver, inner wood frame. *Tachul* (repoussé and chasing). 21.6". *National Museum of Korea*

Lotus-Shaped Incense Burner. NT No. 92. Goryeo dynasty, 1077 CE. Bronze. 8.5". *National Museum of Korea*

Heavenly Landscape of Bronze Mirror. Shin1358. Goryeo dynasty, tenth–eleventh centuries. 8.3". *National Museum of Korea*

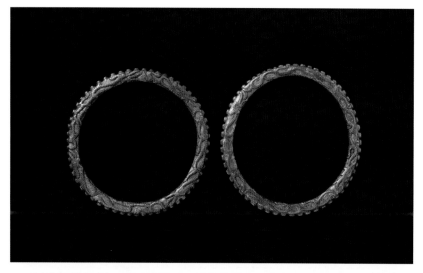

Golden Bracelets. Silla dynasty, early sixth century. Excavated from Noseo-dong No. 215 Tomb. Gold. 3.125". *National Museum of Korea*

Silver Cup with High-Footed Base on Wide Platter. Duk130. Goryeo dynasty, twelfth century. *Tachul* (repoussé and chasing). 4.8". *National Museum of Korea*

Set of Six Golden Bracelets. Silla dynasty, early fifth century. Excavated from Geumgwanchong Tomb. Gold. 3"–3.125". *National Museum of Korea*

Ritual Wine Cup with Handle. Duk3642. Goryeo dynasty, twelfth century. *Tachul* (repoussé and chasing). Silver and gold amalgam. 1.1". *National Museum of Korea*

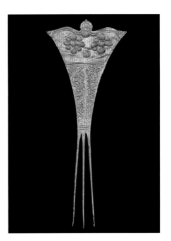

Ghwancha. No. 091-1. Head ornaments for men. Joseon dynasty, 1392–1897 CE. Jade and agate. 0.6"~1.4". *Sookmyung Women's University Museum*

Big Phoenix & Dragon Innocence Burner. NT No. 287. Baekjae dynasty, seventh–eighth centuries. *Tachul.* Gold-plated bronze. 25.2". *Booyoe National Museum*

Queen's Silver Bracelet with Dragon Design & Inscriptions. NT No. 160. Baekjae dynasty, 520 CE. *Tachul* (repoussé and chasing). 3.1". *Gongju National Museum*

King's Gold Chignon Ornament. NT No. 159. Baekjae dynasty, sixth century. Repoussé and chasing, flower and vine designs. 7.2". *Gongju National Museum*

Lock & Key. No. 11-75. Late Joseon dynasty, nineteenth century. *Tachul.* Nickel and brass. 2" × 2" × 0.8". *Collection of Lock Museum*

Sheath with Slit and Loop Handle. No. 39.607. Goryeo dynasty, twelfth–thirteenth centuries. Gilt silver with repoussé decoration. 19.4" × 0.76". *Photograph © 2018 Museum of Fine Arts, Boston*

Horse Decoration. Object. Three Kingdoms period, 57–676 CE. 4.7" × 6.5". *Tokyo National Museum, Japan*

Silver-Plated Arm Bracelet. Bracelet. Goryeo dynasty, twelfth–thirteenth centuries. 3.5" × 2.3". *Tokyo National Museum, Japan*

Gilt Silver Gourd-Shaped Bottle. GM 22. Goryeo dynasty, twelfth–thirteenth centuries. 1.3" × 4.3" × 4.3" (base only). *Collection of Cheonmisa*

Gilt Silver Gourd-Shaped Bottle. GM 22. Goryeo dynasty, twelfth–thirteenth centuries. 4.2" × 2.3" × 2.3" (bottle only). *Collection of Cheonmisa*

Gilt Silver Gourd-Shaped Bottle. GM 22. Bottle with base. Goryeo dynasty, twelfth–thirteenth centuries. 5.1" × 4.3" × 4.3". *Collection of Cheonmisa*

유리지 (劉里知) YOO Lizzy. *Sarira Reliquary II.* Container. 2006–2007. Chasing and repoussé (*tachul*), *jjoi ipsa.* 24K gold, sterling silver, glass. 9.1" × 5.6" × 5.6". *Collection of Yoo Lizzy Metal Crafts Museum*

유리지 (劉里知) YOO Lizzy. *Lake*. Object. 1987. Line inlay (*kkium*), *tachul, keum-boo*. Fine silver, nickel silver. 3.5" × 13.2" × 10.2". *Collection of Yoo Lizzy Metal Crafts Museum*

YOO was interested in combining realistic shapes with geometrically stylized shapes, and selected subjects such as flowers and fishes for the theme of her artworks. For *Lake*, she made the work look like an attractive lake by putting plumped fish onto a metal sheet.

유리지 (劉里知) YOO Lizzy. *Lake* (close-up). *Collection of Yoo Lizzy Metal Crafts Museum*

CHO Sung Hae

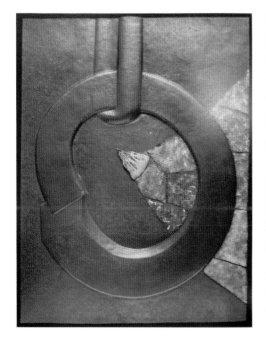

조성혜 (趙星慧) CHO Sung Hae.
Focus. Wall relief. 1991. Chasing
and repoussé (*tachul),* fabricating,
enameling (*chilbo*), coloring, and
patina. Copper, enamel. 3" × 2" ×
0.5".

조성혜 (趙星慧) CHO Sung Hae.
Mother. Wall relief. 2007. Chasing
and repoussé (*tachul*), fabricating,
coloring. Copper, patina. 42.4" ×
28" × 20".

최지은 (崔芝殷) CHOI Jieun. *Hunter III.* Brooch. 2013. Chasing and repoussé *(tachul).* Copper, brass, sterling silver, plating. 4.3" × 3.9" × 2.4".

최지은 (崔芝殷) CHOI Jieun. *Mother and Child.* Brooch. 2014. Chasing and repoussé *(tachul)* and painting. Copper, brass. 4.5" × 3.5" × 1".

Drawing has always been a part of my daily life, so it was natural for me to incorporate some of my drawings into my metalwork. Unlike drawing on a piece of paper, with metal I was able to create depth in the drawings, bringing the design to life.

Once the metal dish was raised and planished, I started outlining the patterns spontaneously with a liner chasing tool as if I was drawing on paper. [The subconscious] is filled with patterns without a clear starting or ending point.

조민희 (趙敏熙) JO Angela Mini.
Subconscious. Platter. 2014.
Tachul, chasing and repoussé.
Copper. 1.2" × 6.3" × 9.5".

정영관 (鄭永琯) JUNG Young Kuwan. *Certain Longing*. Container. 2001. Raising, forming, chasing and repoussé (*tachul*) fabricating, and finishing. Sterling silver. 11.4" × 3" × 3".

정영관 (鄭永琯) JUNG Young Kuwan. *The Quiet Festival*. Teapot. 2009. Raising, forming, chasing and repoussé (*tachul*), carving black wood, riveting, and fabricating finishes. 9.5" × 10.1" × 4.1".

The Quiet Festival is inspired by the pattern of the jug: *kundika* with willow, reed, and waterfowl design, for the clearest water in the Goryeo dynasty of Korea. It emphasizes the beauty of a curved surface through split face with plate work.

KANG Chan Kyun

강찬균 (姜燦均) KANG Chan Kyun, member of the National Academy of the Arts (in Fine Metal Arts) of the Republic of Korea. *A Private Conversation*. Vessel. 1980. Chasing and repoussé (*tachul*), forming, fabricating, and polishing. Nickel silver. 8" × 10.8" × 4".

KANG Hyerim

강혜림 (姜惠林) KANG Hyerim. *Time . . . Fly 1 & 2*. Brooches. 2009. *Tachul*. Sterling silver, Swiss-movement glass, CZ. 2.1" × 2.8" × 0.3"; 2.8" × 2.2" × 0.3".

강혜림 (姜惠林) KANG Hyerim. *Time . . . Blooming*. Brooch. 2009. *Tachul*, chasing and repoussé. Sterling silver, Swiss-movement glass, CZ. 2.8" × 2.2" × 0.3".

강혜림 (姜惠林) KANG Hyerim. *Time = Imagination + Waiting*. Kitchen timer. 2008. Punched-looking cuttings on the bowl, and chasing and repoussé (*tachul*) designs on the top of the bowl as timer. Sterling silver, copper, kitchen timer, aquamarine, and gold plating.

It is very important for me to use certain forms symbolizing 5,000 years of traditional Korean culture. My vessel forms are based on the everyday objects of my surroundings. I am inspired by the curved lines on the protruding corners of *hanok* (Korean home) wooden eaves, socks, a bundle of drying soybean blocks, the sleeves of traditional dress, a grass-roofed house, drums, or the rounded ridge of a mountain.

I produce all sections by raising, forming, *tachul*, and forging, constructing thick wires for the top rim and side elements.

김종렬 (金鍾烈) KIM Chong Ryul. *Bracelet I, II, III.* 1989. Forming, constructing, and Korean repoussé and chasing (*tachul*). Sterling silver, copper, nickel silver. 1.2" × 3.32" × 3.32"; 1.2" × 3.32" × 3.32"; 1.6" × 3.4" × 3.4".

김종렬 (金鍾烈) KIM Chong Ryul. *Trace.* Vessel. 1989. Forming, raising, forging, constructing, and Korean repoussé and chasing (*tachul*). Copper, brass, nickel silver. 8.4" × 8.4" × 8.4".

김종렬 (金鍾烈) KIM Chong Ryul. *The Scent of Tradition 1.* Container. 1986. Forming, raising, forging, construction, Korean repoussé and chasing (*tachul*). Copper, nickel silver. 10" × 13.6" × 13.6".

김종렬 (金鍾烈) KIM Chong Ryul. *The Scent of Tradition 2*. Vessel. 1989. Forming, raising, forging, fabricating, Korean chasing and repoussé (*tachul*). Copper, patina, hand-woven rice-straw mat. 6.8" × 14.8" × 11.2".

KIM Sanghoon

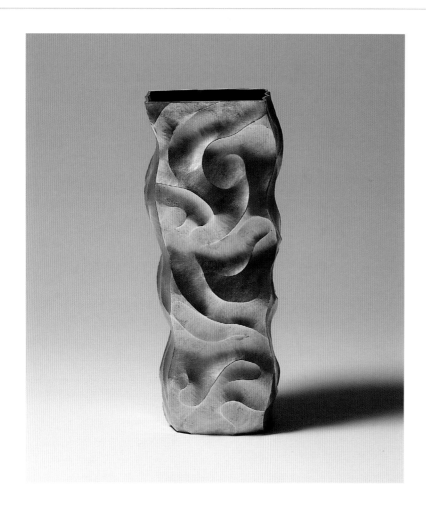

김상훈 KIM Sanghoon. *Memoir Drips*. Vessel. 2016. Chasing and repoussé (*tachul*), constructed, and patina. Brass. 9" × 4.3" × 4.3". My inspiration comes from traveling to unfamiliar places and experiencing the rich variety of the natural world. The multiple layers in this vessel represent the moments of my life accumulating over time.

김영옥 (金榮玉) KIM Youngock. *Thistle Set.* Teapot, two cups, and two saucers on a tray. 2015. Raising, chasing and repoussé (*tachul*), forming, fabricating, finishing, Rhinoceros 3-D, cast and fiber-string macramé wrapping over the handle. Fine and sterling silver. Teapot: 10.4" × 6.8" × 4"; tray: 1.2" × 15.2" × 5.6"; saucers: 0.5" × 1.6" × 1.6" each.

    Thistle Set was created with a contemporary variation of the traditional *tachul* (chasing and repoussé) method. A wooden mold was carved to hammer wavy patterns into the metal instead of hammering on pitch. The ornamental patterns at the end of the teapot handles and the top of the lid were created using the Rhinoceros 3-D program and cast, to use as ornament multiples. *Thistle Set* is the product of combined traditional and contemporary techniques.

KWAK Soonhwa

곽순화 (郭順華) KWAK Soonhwa.
Pine Tree Forest. Wall relief. 2013.
Tachul (chasing and repoussé) and
ottchil. Copper, mother-of-pearl,
ottchil. 36.4" × 28.4" × 2.8".

RYU Ki Hyun

유기현 (柳基鉉) RYU Ki Hyun.
Dano Backstage. Wall relief. 2002.
Chasing and repoussé (*tachul*),
forming, fabricating, and patina.
Sterling silver. 13.8" × 9.4" × 1.9".

유기현 (柳基鉉) RYU Ki Hyun.
Wealth. Wall relief. 2002. Chasing
and repoussé (*tachul*), forming,
fabricating, and patina. Sterling
silver. 10.6" × 4.3" × 0.4".

RYU Yeunhee

류연희 (柳延熹) RYU Yeunhee. *Paperweights*. Paperweight containers for ink-stone water calligraphy article. 2005 *Tachul* (chasing and repoussé) on silver, connected with silver thread and finished with *chilbo* enameling. Gold, silver, copper, *kuromido*, stone. 3"–7" × 2"–4"; 2"–5".

SEO Dosik

서도식 (徐道植) SEO Dosik. *Pumpkin*. Oil lamp. 1994. Raising, forming, planishing, forming, chasing and repoussé (*tachul*), fabricating, patina, and wax finishing. Copper, patina. 6.8" × 8" × 8".

CHAPTER 5

Lacquering and Mother-of-Pearl Overlay (*Ottchil* and *Najeon Ottchil*)

Traditionally, *ottchil* or lacquering with sumac sap was used by the Chinese, Japanese, and Koreans as a preservative coating on metal and wooden utilitarian objects. Sumac trees are common in Korea, and since the third century, *ottchil* has been used to decorate sword handles. In modern times this technique is used for art objects.

Ottchil use started in the Bronze Age, and mother-of-pearl inlay work (nacre inlay on *ottchil*) began at the end of the Silla dynasty and the beginning of the Goryeo dynasty (seventh to eighth centuries).

For the thousand years since the Goryeo dynasty, mother-of-pearl has captivated viewers' imaginations through its natural shine and iridescent colors. Among Asian countries, only the Koreans used mother-of-pearl inlay on *ottchil* (called *najeon chil*). In the Joseon dynasty (fourteenth to the early twentieth century), this mother-of-pearl inlay on the *ottchil* became well established in the royal courts through its use on small chests of drawers, flower vases, treasure boxes, small portable tables, and the ornamental plates called *najeon chilggi*.

Ottchil is produced in Korea, China, Japan, Myanmar, and Vietnam. When the *ot* (sumac) tree, *Rhus verniciflua*, is cut, the *ottchil* sap flows. The raw liquid is placed in a container at 100°F–113°F (38°C–45°C) and stirred frequently for a period of several hours. This preliminary liquid is called *ssangchil*. Later purification steps, including the addition of terrapin oil or pigments, produce purified *ottchil* called *jeongjechil*.

Today, *ottchil* coatings are used on furniture, eating implements, and vessels to keep material from being exposed to air, acid, and other chemicals. Although the raw sap can cause contact allergies, the cured *ottchil* is environmentally friendly and provides long-term protection from decay and acid.

Contemporary artists coat a variety of materials with *ottchil*: Korean rice paper, soybean-paste-coated waxed paper or cotton/hemp cloth, mild steel, aluminum, copper, silver, brass, and wood. They create hollowares that hold food to eat, wearable ornaments, and various other objects.

Black Lacquer Box with Mother-of-Pearl Decoration and Flower and Bird Design. No. 92. Box. Joseon dynasty, nineteenth century. Mother-of-pearl, *ottchil*, and wood. 3.8" × 11.2" × 11.2". *Koryo Museum, Kyoto, Japan*

Peony Butterfly Box. TH-350. Joseon dynasty, seventeenth–eighteenth centuries. 3.3" × 10.2" × 2.4". *Tokyo National Museum, Japan*

Flower-Shaped Box with Stylized Chrysanthemums. No. 34.69a–34.69b. Goryeo dynasty, thirteenth–fourteenth centuries. Lacquered wood inlaid with mother-of-pearl and painted tortoiseshell *ottchil*. 1.75" × 4.5". *Photograph © 2018 Museum of Fine Arts, Boston*

Craftsperson
Technical References

KIM Sungsoo

Director of Tongyeong Ottchil Museum & Art Center, Master of *Ottchil* and *Najeon Ottchil* of Arts and Crafts.

김성수 (金聖洙) KIM Sungsoo, Master of *Najeon* and *Ottchil* Crafts Artist. *Octagonal Jeumiimoon Box.* 1990. Aluminum, wood powder, *ottchil* on wood. 22" × 11" × 11". *Tongyeong Ottchil Museum Collection*

김성수 (金聖洙) KIM Sungsoo, Master of *Najeon* and *Ottchil* Crafts Artist. *Acacia Single Deck Chest.* 1986. Aluminum, wood powder, *ottchil* on wood. 42" × 18" × 18". *Tongyeong Ottchil Museum Collection*

김성수 (金聖洙) KIM Sungsoo,
Master of *Najeon* and *Ottchil* Crafts
Artist. *Smilax*. Vase. 1986.
Aluminum, wood powder, *ottchil* on
wood. 8" × 8" × 8". *Tongyeong
Ottchil Museum Collection*

Lacquering (*Ottchil*) Demonstration by YUN Sanghee

Materials:
table
glass plate
wood plate
stone (or marble) plate
gwei-yahl (special brushes for *ottchil* application)
scoops (spatulas)
whetstones
knives

Basic *ottchil* ingredients needed:
ssengchil (*ottchil* that has been cleaned only once)

heukchil ottchil (mixed with black coloring chemical agent)
color *ottchil*
terrapin oil (for diluting *ottchil*)
Carborundum sanding papers
charcoal for fine sanding
polishing compounds (Brasso, Amore, polishing powder compound)

Application of Korean oriental lacquer, *ottchil*, to metal and ceramic surfaces requires a different process than it does for application of *ottchil* to wood, fabric, leather, or plastic surfaces. For metal and ceramic surfaces, the lacquer must be cured in an electric kiln.

Baekgoal (Wood Object Prior to *Ottchil* Application) by YUN Sanghee

1. *Baekgoal* surface preparation: Use #180–320 carborundum paper and clean under running water. Clean further in the diluted acetic acid pickle, wash, and dry well.
2. *Ssengchil* application: Apply a 7:3 ratio of *ssengchil* to terrapin oil.
3. Place in the electric kiln at 356°F (180°C) for one to two hours and cool.
4. *Ssengchil* surface cleaning: sand the surface with #320–600 paper.
5. Apply a 7:3 ratio of *ssengchil* to terrapin oil and cure well.
6. Bake in the cold electric kiln and set the temperature at 320°F (150°C) for 1–1.5 hours. Take it out when it is cold.
7. Sand the surface with #400–600 paper.
8. *Heukchil* (black *ottchil*) must be applied in a 6:4 ratio of black *ottchil* to terrapin oil.
9. Each application must be cured in the curing cabinet, ideally made with Japanese *hinoki* cypress for natural dehydration for more than 12–24 hours at 66°F–77°F (20°C–25°C) with adequate humidity.
10. *Joongchil* (color *ottchil*): apply a 7:3 ratio of colored *ottchil* to terrapin oil. Each step must be cured in the cabinet.
11. Final *ssengchil*: Final color application should be in a clean, enclosed room with no dust. Use the curing cabinet to dry.

Keumtaechil: Process of *Ottchil* Application on Bare Metal Object by YUN Sanghee

1. Metal surface preparation: Use #180–320 carborundum paper and clean under running water. Clean further in the diluted acetic acid pickle, wash, and dry well. The surface must be roughened in order for the ottchil to bind onto it.

2. Mix *ssengchil* (*ottchil* that has been cleaned only once) and dilute terrapin agent at 3:1 ratio. Paint with a clean brush. It is important to wear gloves due to potential irritations and/or severe allergic reactions from the *ottchil*.

3. Apply the first application at 356°F (180°C) for one to two hours in the electric kiln or with a torch.

4. The coloring should be dark brown, which indicates a good curing.

5. *Ssengchil* metal surface cleaning: Sand the surface of the object with #320–600 paper. Repeat steps 2, 3, and 4 twice. Apply 7:3 ratio of *ssengchil* to terrapin oil and cure well. The second application must cure at 320°F–356°F (150°C–180°C) for 1–1.5 hours.

6. Each application must be cured in the curing cabinet, ideally made with Japanese *hinoki* cypress for natural dehydration for more than 12–24 hours at 66°F–77°F (20°C–25°C) with adequate humidity.

7. *Heukchil* (black *ottchil*) must be applied in a 6:4 ratio of black *ottchil* to terrapin oil. Each step must be cured in the cabinet.

8. If you want a variety of colors, you can apply the desired color after black *ottchil*. Apply a 7:3 ratio of colored *ottchil* to terrapin oil. Each step must dry in the *ottchil* cabinet, and final color application should be in a clean, enclosed room with no dust. Use cabinet to dry.

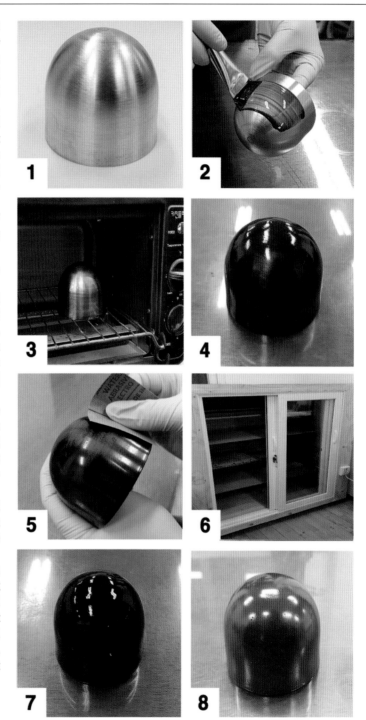

윤상희 (尹祥熙) YUN Sanghee.
Attack by Green Horns. Neck piece.
2009. *Moksimjeopl ottchil*, wood,
sterling silver, gold plating, 24K
gold leaf. 2.9" × 22.5" × 9.8".

윤상희 (尹祥熙) YUN Sanghee. *I Am a Super Mom in My Thirtieth*. Vessel with lid. 2016-2017. 3-D printing, *ottchil* (Korean lacquer), hemp cloth, mother-of-pearl, ABS, brass, gold plating, bean curd, gold leaf. 19" × 28" × 11".

CHO Hyunsoo

Demonstration of *Ottchil* on Tall Vase by CHO Hyunsoo

1. Create the object as your preferred shape and clean it to completely remove oil.
2. Coat the surface and inside of the object with the primary refined *ottchil*.
3. Bake in the electric furnace and process the primary hardening for 2 hours at 150°C (320°F).
4. Coat with the secondary refined *ottchil*. Wait for 30 minutes and spray mother-of-pearl powder.
5. Bake in the electric furnace and process the secondary high temperature for hardening.
6. Paint the object with refined *ottchil* for a third time. After drying, insert it into the electric furnace and process at a high temperature for hardening. Repeat this process twice.
7. Paint the object with colored *ottchil* (1:1 ratio between refined *ottchil* and colored *ottchil*) according to the design, insert it into the electric furnace (60%–70%), and process at a high temperature for hardening.
8. Double paint the object with colored *ottchil* according to the design.
9. Dry the object in the Japanese *Hinoki* or cypress cabinet and let it dehydrate for more than 6 hours at 20–25°C (68–77°F) with adequate humidity.
10. Repeatedly paint the object with colored *ottchil* according to the design and insert it into the drying cabinet for natural dehydration.
11. Use #400 DIA blocks to polish the uneven surface created due to mother-of-pearl powder. Remove the hole created due to the overlapping mother-of-pearl and make sure that the formed patterns are not too compact.
12. Paint the object twice with white-colored *ottchil*, twice with orange-colored ottchil, three times with yellow-colored *ottchil* and three times with brown-colored *ottchil* according to the design. Then, insert it into the drying cabinet again for natural dehydration.
13. Use a rough scrubber to grind the entire surface. This helps to adhere the *ottchil* coating prior to the processing *ottchil* coating.
14. When the coating process is complete, Use #400/#600 DIA blocks to grind the entire surface.
15. Grind the entire surface with water and fine whetstones in the order of #800, #1000, #1200, and #1500 to even the surface and form patterns.
16. Apply the exclusive *ottchil* coating compound to a cotton cloth and use this cloth to polish the object.
17. According to the design and pattern, use polishes with Amor polisher for the final polishing.

조현수 (曺賢洙) CHO Hyunsoo. *Contain*. Vessel. 2017. Raising, forming, polishing, lacquering, and nacre (mother-of-pearl overlaying) on *ottchil* (sumac lacquering). Copper, *ottchil*, nacre (mother-of-pearl). 11.8" × 9.4" × 9.4". *Photo, artist*

Ottchil Work Process Without a Drying Cabinet (Using Styrofoam Box), by CHO Hyunsoo

1. Thoroughly wash the surface of the product with a coarse scrubber and neutral detergent.
2. Apply refined color lacquer evenly to the surface of the object
3. If you don't have access to an electric furnace, use a household oven. Preheat the oven to 356°F (180°C) and bake for 30 minutes.
4. To increase the adhesion of the lacquer, scratch the surface evenly with a coarse scrubber.
5. Apply refined color lacquer again.
6. After 30 minutes of lacquering, spray the mother-of-pearl powder when adhesion is good.
7. Bake in the oven at 356°F (180°C) for 30 minutes.
8. Apply lacquer well and spray again with mother-of-pearl powder and bake at 356°F (180°C) for 30 minutes.
9. Apply color lacquer to the surface again.
10. If you don't have access to a *chiljang* (drying cabinet), put a sponge soaked in water in a Styrofoam box and check inside the box with a digital thermometer/

hygrometer. Optimum natural drying conditions are a temperature of ±77°F (25°C) and a humidity of ±65 percent.
11. Make sure the sponge is soaked with water, and put both the lacquered object and sponge into the Styrofoam box. Let it dry naturally. When it is completely dried, apply the same color lacquer again and repeat the natural drying.
12. Apply a different color of lacquer to create a colored pattern.
13. Dry the object in the Styrofoam box again. When it is completely dried, apply the same color of lacquer again and repeat the natural drying process twice.
14. When lacquer work is complete, polish the entire surface using DIA block sandpaper of #400 and #600.
15. Moisten the fine grindstone with water and make color patterns in the order of #800, #1000, #1200, and #1500.
16. Apply lacquer-only compound onto a soft cloth for the first polish.
17. Finish with a polish to ensure that the color of the intended pattern is visible.

조현수 (曺賢洙) CHO Hyunsoo. *A Cup.* Cup. 2018. Sumac lacquering (*ottchil*) and nacre (mother-of-pearl) overlay. Fine silver, sumac lacquer (*ottchil*), nacre (mother-of-pearl), polishing compound, and final coating wax. 2.3" × 1.9" × 1.9" (demo piece). *Photo, artist*

조현수 (曺賢洙) CHO Hyunsoo. *Special Day*. Bowl with lid. 2014. Raising, forming, polishing, lacquering, and nacre (mother of pearl overlaying) on *ottchil* (sumac lacquering). Bronze (78% copper, 22% tin), lacquerware. 3.2" × 3.7" × 3.7". *Photo, artist*

조현수 (曺賢洙) CHO Hyunsoo. *Two of Us*. Cups. 2014. Raising, forming, polishing, lacquering, and nacre (mother-of-pearl overlaying) on *ottchil* (sumac lacquering). Bronze (78% copper, 22% tin), lacquer, nacre (mother-of-pearl). 2.1" × 2" × 2" each. *Photo, artist*

Making *Sanhwa Chul* (Adding Oxidation on Iron) on Metal Surface before Applying *Ottchil*, by KWAK Soonhwa

1. Coat the metal surface with *sanhwa chul* (oxidized iron-powder mixed with *ottchil*) and cure. The metalwork is cured in an electric furnace for 30 minutes at 302°F (150°C). The torch method may also be used.
2. Apply the black pigment *ottchil* (*heukchil*: *ottchil* mixed with black coloring chemical agent) or black color lacquer (*ottchil*) onto the background and apply mother-of-pearl in cut strips with *tachul* (chasing and repoussé) process. These were used for detailed expressions as silhouettes.
3. After the mother-of-pearl overlay is dried, color *juhap* (well-refined *ottchil*) and cure in the curing cabinet.
4. To reveal the mother-of-pearl decoration, sand the surface with sandpaper.
5. Add the final color of *ottchil* on the background and dry in a curing cabinet.
6. Finalize surface with high polish.

Demonstration of *Geumchil* (24K Gold Powder Painting) Technique by KWAK Soonhwa

Ottchil works best when the temperature is at 68°F–77°F (20°C–25°C) with 60–70 percent humidity.

Technique 1: Direct *Geumchil* (24K gold powder) Application
1. Apply *ssangchil* (unrefined *ottchil*) to the specific area.
2. Buff off only the areas of *ssangchil* application with rayon cloths until the surface is slightly sticky.
3. Spread *geumchil* (gold powder) lightly and evenly with a brush or a cotton ball.
4. Brush off excess gold powder with a soft brush.
5. Dry the whole object for at least a day or until the surface feels completely dry.

Technique 2:
1. Apply *juhap* (refined *ottchil*, also called *jeongjechil*) to the specific area.
2. Apply *geumchil* when the *juhap* feels slightly sticky.

   Rainy days or seasons with lots of humidity will cure the piece in about three to six hours in the curing closet with the right temperatures. However, sunny days with less humidity will require the piece to be kept overnight to become tacky enough to apply the gold powder.
3. When the surface feels slightly sticky, spread *geumchil* evenly with a brush or cotton ball.
4. When the surface feels completely dry, brush off *geumchil* with a dry painting brush or large shoeshine brush.
5. Cure completely to finish the work.

곽순화 (郭順華) KWAK Soonhwa. *An Innocent Smile*. Wall relief. 2014. *Ottchil*, *keumchil* (24K gold powder painting) and *tachul* techniques. Aluminum, mother-of-pearl, *ottchil*. 1.6" × 27.4" × 36".

This wall relief represents Korea's treasure Pensive Bodhisattva (*Mirukbangasayusang*), on a bronze panel.

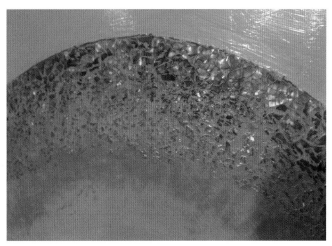

곽순화 (郭順華) KWAK Soonhwa. *An Innocent Smile* (close-up).

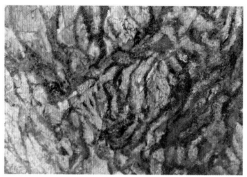

곽순화 (郭順華) KWAK Soonhwa. *Manmulsang*. Vessel. 2016. Iron, *ottchil*, mother-of-pearl. 16" × 15.7" × 15.7".

This vessel represents the Manmulsang rocks of Geumgang Mountain and is decorated with *ottchil* and mother-of-pearl (*najoenchil*) overlay on its moon shape. The form was spun shaped, and oxidized steel lacquer (*sanhwa chul ottchil*) was brushed on before it was baked in an electric furnace for 30 minutes at 130°C. All surfaces are decorated with several processes of lacquers and mother-of-pearl application.

곽순화 (郭順華) KWAK Soonhwa. *Big Pine Tree*. Vessel. 2016. Spun raised iron vessel, applied *sanhwa chul ottchil*, and mother-of-pearl overlay on the vessel. 16.8" × 16" × 16".

곽순화 (郭順華) KWAK Soonhwa. *Mountain Seolack*. Wall relief. 2015. *Ottchil*. Aluminum, lacquer, mother-of-pearl. 36" × 46.8" × 1".

Traditional and Contemporary Combination: Sumac Lacquering and Mother-of-Pearl Overlaying (*Ottchil* and *Najeonchil*), by KIM Hyunju

1. *Ottchil* (lacquer) mixing, spreading, and coating: Lacquer liquid, *ottchil* (sumac sap), is carefully applied on the sanded metal surface in an even layer with a metal spatula. The surface is stroked repeatedly to remove any air bubbles that develop.

2. *Keumtaechil*: The process of lacquering, or application of *ottchil* to a bare-sanded metal surface in order to prepare for the mother-of-pearl overlay. This process helps inlay mother-of-pearl by acting as glue. Lacquering also prevents deformation and adds stability. It protects the metal surface from tarnish, corrosion, and discoloration, as well as protecting the object against damage from aging, food, or other substances.

3. Heat curing: The object must cure (in a pine wood cabinet preferably made of *hinoki* cypress or hemp wood) at a constant temperature of 64°F–77°F (18°C–25°C) and 60–80 percent humidity.

   This curing process is repeated three times, either in the electric kiln or by torch. The stabilized lacquer coating on the metal provides a waterproof, insect-proof, and airproof surface that is receptive to the addition of other colors or substances, such as mother-of-pearl.

4. *Kkeunneumjil* (cutting/slicing mother-of-pearl strip by strip): Lacquerware inlaid with the brilliant natural colors of mother-of-pearl is called *najeonchil*, which has been a traditional craft in Korean culture since the Goryeo dynasty (918–1392 CE). The technique *kkeunneumjil* requires narrow, small pieces of selected mother-of-pearl, which are applied strip by strip to create a continuous design. It brings out a radiant brilliance and timeless appearance to the work.

5. Gluing and ironing: Mother-of-pearl is glued with animal gelatin glue and is then ironed (process called *jagae butchim* or *jagae gigim*). Ironing and searing the freshly glued mother-of-pearl patterns ensures security.

Ahgyopull, commercially bought cow-bone-gelatin glue (*ahgyopull*), is softened in the double boiler or with "quick size" on the *ottchil* metal surface as the gluing progresses.

Cover mother-of-pearl patterns with a paper towel and apply by using a light portable iron. After ironing is complete, wipe off any excess glue that may have smeared from the mother-of-pearl patterns. Rub off the excess glue with heated water between 194°F and 212°F (90°C–100°C). This process is called "glue removing" (*pullppeggi*), or "sizing removing" (*ahgyopull-ppeggi*).

김현주 (金賢珠) KIM Hyunju. *Draw a Circle 4.* Bowl. 2016. Mother-of-pearl application to bare metal surface (*keumtaechil*), mother-of-pearl overlaying (*jagaechil*), cutting strips of mother-of-pearl (*keuneumjil*), sumac lacquering (*ottchil*). Brass, mother-of-pearl. 7.8" × 11" × 11".

I believe that mother-of-pearl, which retains the shine of the sea, permeates metal in a special way. Creating mother-of-pearl overlay vessels has captivated my imagination through its natural shine and iridescent colors. This traditional material, nacre, a secret science of the shiny pearl, is crucial for my projects combining old and contemporary art practice. This traditional technique becomes my vehicle of communicating between the traditional and the contemporary. It is also more beautiful than using jewels in my artwork.

김현주 (金賢珠) KIM Hyunju. *Draw a Circle 1*. Lamp. 2011. Marriage-of-metals inlay (*jeoul ipsa*), mother-of-pearl application to bare metal surface (*keumtaechil*), mother-of-pearl overlaying (*jagaechil*), cutting strips of mother-of-pearl (*keuneumjil*), sumac lacquering (*ottchil*). Silver, copper, mother-of-pearl. 11" × 6.5" × 6.5".

김현주 (金賢珠) KIM Hyunju. *Draw a Circle 2*. Lamp. 2012. Mother-of-pearl application to bare metal surface (*keumtaechil*), mother-of-pearl overlaying (*jagaechil*), cutting strips of mother-of-pearl (*keuneumjil*), sumac lacquering (*ottchil*). Copper, mother-of-pearl. 8.5" × 6.5" × 6.5".

Ottchil Technique with Hemp Cloth Jewelry by SHIN Heekyung

1. Fill the loosely woven structure of the hemp cloth with a wet paste mixture of *tobun* (fine red clay powder). The mixture should have the consistency of slush. Shake well before use.
2. Glue two hemp cloths by using a mixture of glutinous sweet-rice porridge paste and *ottchil* (ratio of 7:3). Make the porridge paste with approximately 5 tablespoons of sweet rice powder and 1 cup of water. Cook slowly over the stove, stirring constantly to avoid burning, until the paste becomes very clear (same as making laundry starch) and store in the refrigerator for further use.
3. Soak the first layers of hemp cloth in the mixture and cure at 68°F–86°F (20°C–30°C) with 70–85 percent humidity.

   A curing chamber can be made from a corrugated box partially filled with wet newspapers (or a damp sponge). For a more permanent chamber, a wooden cabinet can be manufactured.

   A wooden *ottchil* curing cabinet will give the same curing environment regardless of the season. It is recommended to use Japanese cedar wood (*sugi*) or Korean cedar (*samnamu*), which can withstand high humidity.
4. Apply *ottchil* and cure in the desired box or cabinet. After applying the *tobun* (fine red clay powder) mixture once, apply *ottchil* to strengthen the adhesion. After each application is cured, the surface of the objects has to be sanded with emery paper.
5. *Ottchil* is applied to the hemp cloth until the desired thickness is achieved.
6. Apply lacquer.

   (a) Base *ottchil* process (lacquering): Apply to the cloth until it is stiff and malleable enough to form your desired shape. Use #220 to #600 emery paper for polishing.

   (b) Middle lacquering: create a base with transparent lacquer and polish with #600 to #1000 emery paper.

   (c) Top layer of lacquering: Add desired color to transparent *ottchil* in the form of paint. The number of brushstrokes should be kept to a minimum to keep smoothness. Polish the surface with #1000 to #1200 emery paper.

7. Join the *ottchil* hemp cloth structure to the silver elements of the jewelry piece by riveting.

Jitae Ottchil Technique: *Ottchil* with Korean Rice Paper, by SHIN Heekyung

1. Soak layers of Korean rice paper, using a mixture of glutinous sweet-rice porridge paste and *ottchil* (ratio of 7:3). Cure the soaked rice paper.
2. Add a layer of glutinous rice paste and *ottchil* (ratio of 7:3).
3. Cure before beginning *ottchil* applications. Each *ottchil* layer should be left to cure in the cabinet before the next layer is added. Polish the surface with emery paper before the next layer is applied, until the desired thickness is achieved.
4. Apply lacquer.

   (a) Base *ottchil* process (lacquering): glue to form the shape and use #220 to #600 emery paper for polishing.

   (b) Middle lacquering: create a base with transparent lacquer and polish with #600 to #1000 emery paper.

   (c) Top layer of lacquering: Add desired color to transparent *ottchil* in the form of paint. The number of brushstrokes should be kept to a minimum to keep smoothness. Polish the surface with #1000 to #1200 emery paper.

5. Join the *ottchil* paper structures to silver parts by riveting to finish the jewelry.

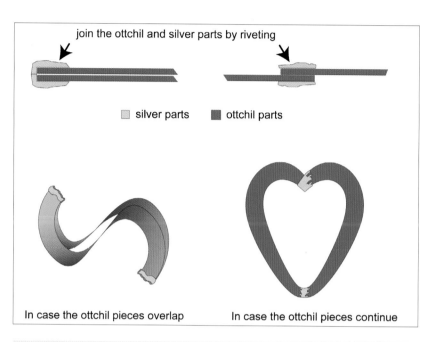

join the ottchil and silver parts by riveting

◻ silver parts   ◼ ottchil parts

In case the ottchil pieces overlap   In case the ottchil pieces continue

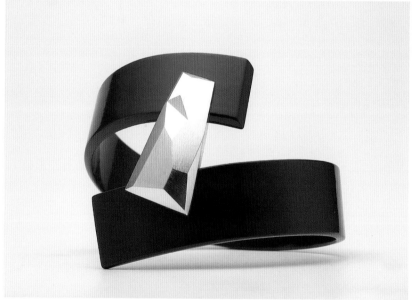

신희경 (申喜卿) SHIN Heekyung.
Block. Bracelet. 2010. Lacquering
on Korean rice paper (*jitaechil*).
Ottchil, Korean rice paper, sterling
silver. 2.4" × 3" × 3".

신희경 (申喜卿) SHIN Heekyung.
Wave 0801. Neck piece. 2008.
Lacquering on Korean rice paper
(*jitaechil*). *Ottchil,* Korean rice paper,
sterling silver. 2.6" × 9.2" × 9.2".

신희경 (申喜卿) SHIN Heekyung.
A Sprout. Ring. 2010. Lacquering
on Korean rice paper (*zitae-chil*).
Ottchil, Korean rice paper, sterling
silver, pearl. 1.6" × 1.72" × 1.08".

CHUNG Eunmee

In my work I deal with cancer and environmental issues. I believe that current issues involving environmental sustainability and nature can be greatly affected by the awakened minds of artists. Creating jewelry with a traditional Korean coloring of *ottchil* elaborates on an artistic sense sustainable both to east and west.

정은미 (鄭恩美) CHUNG Eunmee. *Cancer #3*. Brooch. 2008. Fabricated. Sterling silver, cotton-mâché, *ottchil* powder. 4" × 4" × 0.5".

정은미 (鄭恩美) CHUNG Eunmee. *Flying Stillness*. Necklace. 2014. Fabricated. Steel, *ottchil*. 14" × 10" × 1".

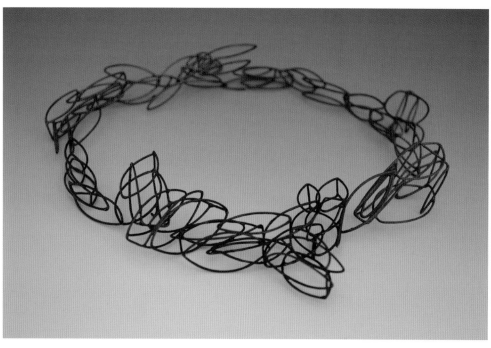

JEONG Sejin

The ancient Korean lacquer technique (*ottchil*) is both preservative and decorative. Its use in my pieces expresses longevity. Creating an *ottchil* surface decoration is a lengthy procedure which contrasts sharply with the contemporary use of rapid production methods. This synthetic resin ring was created using 3-D printing and then followed by a slow *ottchil* coloration. The "Little Apple" merges modern and ancient techniques and exploits the vivid colors possible with *ottchil* to illustrate the tempting beauty of an apple.

정세진 (鄭世珍) JEONG Sejin.
He Handed Me a Little Apple.
2013. Diamond, electroformed copper, gold plated, Korean lacquer. 1.5" × 0.9" × 0.9".

KOH Heeseung

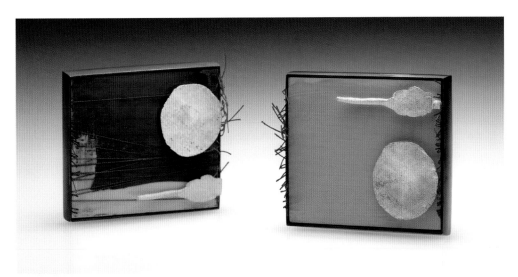

고희승 (高嬉丞) KOH Heeseung.
Balance. Brooches. 2009. *Ottchil* painting. Sterling silver, wood, thread, *ottchil.* 1.85" × 1.65" × 0.27" each.

김춘봉 (金春逢) KIM Choon
Bong. *Tea Tray and Teapot*.
Lacquerware. Copper, tin.
6.3" × 4.7" × 5.5"; 2" × 7" × 7".

김춘봉 (金春逢) KIM Choon
Bong. *Teapot*. Lacquerware.
Copper, tin. 6.3" × 4.7" × 5.5".

LEE, Martha Seungwon

My artwork concentrates on exploring the harmony of function, form, structure, shape, and material in traditional metalsmithing. Since 1998, I have used *ottchil* application to enhance my silversmithing vessels and other ornamental work.

이승원 (李勝媛) LEE, Martha Seungwon. *Pot.* Object. 1999. Silver, *ottchil*, silk thread, acrylic. 7.4" × 15.3" × 2.8".

이승원 (李勝媛) LEE, Martha Seungwon. *Pot.* Object. 2011. Silver, *ottchil*, silk thread, acrylic, poly. 6" × 15" × 3".

LIM Sujin

임수진 (林受珍) LIM Sujin. *Layered.* Brooches. 2016. *Ottchil* on walnut wood, sterling silver. 2.4" × 2.4" × 0.2" each.

Harmony is created with the combination of various colors along with the balance of colors, wood, and metal. The *ottchil* technique of layering and drying represents the flow of time.

NOH Kyungju

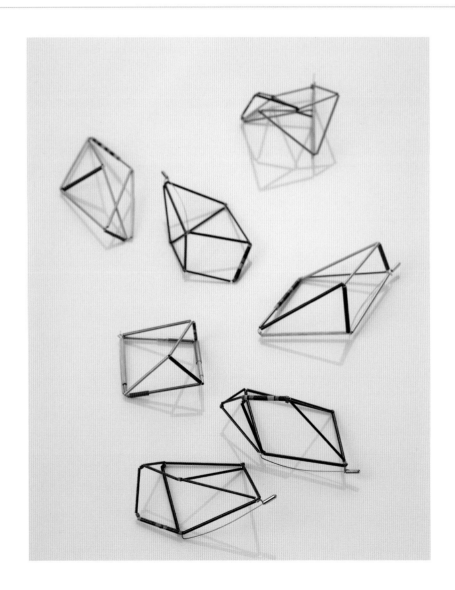

노경주(盧暻主) NOH Kyungju. *3D Bracelets.* Bracelets. 2016. *Ottchil.* Brass tubing, sterling-silver beads, stainless-steel wire, *ottchil.* Variable sizes. 2" × 3" × 1".

My jewelry pieces are practical, with a modern geometric shape and traditional lacquer colors. They are lightweight and have a structure that changes freely.

김홍자 (金弘子) OKIM Komelia
Hongja. *Women's Tale 1 & 2.*
Memory containers. 2012–2017.
These vessels represent women in
conversation and can contain their
stories or memories. Sinking,
raising, forming, fabricating,
oxidizing, shading, and sumac
ottchil. Fine and sterling silver,
Korean lacquer. 38" × 27" × 10";
37" × 22" × 10".

For years I have utilized the traditional Korean lacquering technique of *ottchil* on metal, which has been effective in removing environmental and health hazards. Moreover, combining traditional methods and contemporary usages of adding hemp cords and painting with several *ottchil* colors has brought out warmth and deeper aesthetic sensitivities in my work.

서도식 (徐道植) SEO Dosik. *Persimmon II*. Vessel. 2010. Sinking, raising, forming, fabricating, Korean lacquer coloring (*ottchil*) finish. Silver, lacquer. 1.6" × 12.8" × 12.8"; 3.2" (top view).

서도식 (徐道植) SEO Dosik. *Sunrise and Sunset*. Vessels. 2016. Raising, texturing, forming and adding hemp cords, Korean lacquer (*ottchil*) coloring finish. Copper, hemp cord, lacquer (*ottchil*). 12" × 14.4" × 14.4"; 10.8" × 13.6" × 13.6".

서도식 (徐道植) SEO Dosik. *Work 2*. Platter with persimmon. 2003. Raising, sinking, forming, assembling, fabricating, several *ottchil* coloring finish. Copper, lacquer (*ottchil*). 2.8" × 12.8" × 12.8".

손계연 (孫係蓮) SON Kye-Yeon.
Innatus Forma 2017-1. Object.
2017. Forming and constructing
with micro-arc-weld, Korean
lacquer (*ottchil*) coloring; five layers
of different Korean lacquer (*ot*)
colors were applied to achieve
delicate color differences, water
resistance, and anti-corrosion for
finishing. Steel, Korean lacquer.
14" × 6.5" × 5.5".

손계연 (孫係蓮) SON Kye-Yeon.
Innatus Forma 2017-2. Object.
2017. Six layers of different
Korean lacquer (*ot*) colors were
applied on hammer-textured
copper cylinder. Copper, Korean
lacquer. 34" × 4.5" × 4.5".

SONG Kwangja, Designer

The open, smooth, and overflowing shapes of the candleholders, flower bowls, and tray convey my intention of openness and free-flowing conversation among family members and friends gathered around the dinner table. They convey a closeness, intimate, and aesthetically inviting setting.

송광자 (宋光子) SONG Kwangja, designer. *Sharing Platter with Tray.* 2016. Walnut tray is carved and textured, and the sterling-silver platter is raised by sinking raising, forming, finishing, and gold-colored lacquering (*keumchil ottchil*) finish. Walnut, sterling silver, gold-colored lacquer (*keumchil ottchil*). 2" × 34" × 12"; 1.6" × 32" × 11.3".

송광자 (宋光子) SONG Kwangja, designer. *Flower Bowl I.* 2015. *Ottchil.* Sterling silver, Korean lacquer. 2.4" × 13.5" × 6". Raising, forming, shaping, refining, fabricating, lacquering (*ottchil*).

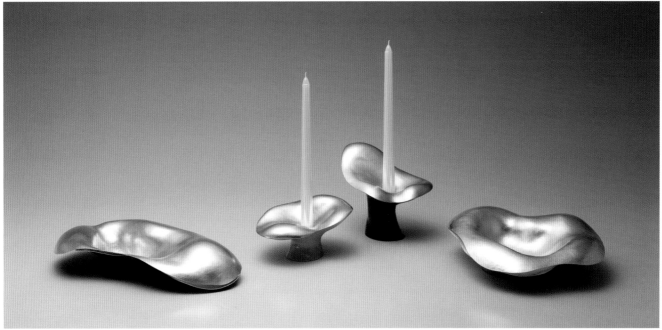

송광자 (宋光子) SONG Kwangja, designer.*Candle-Holding Bowls I, II.* 2015. *Ottchil.* Sterling silver, Korean lacquer. 6" × 8" × 5.6" and 3.5" × 7" × 5". Raising, forming, shaping, refining, fabricating, lacquering (*ottchil*).

송광자 (宋光子) SONG Kwangja, designer. *Conversation: Table Setting with Set of Candle Holders I & II and Flower Bowls I & II.* 2007, 2015. *Ottchil.* Sterling silver, Korean lacquer. 14.5" × 18.5" × 14" each; 8" × 17" × 12" each.

Surface Color Applications

Enameling (*Chilbo*)

"Seven treasures" is the direct translation of *chilbo* (enameling). This technique was introduced from China through the Silk Road and became popular during the Three Kingdoms period (57–676 CE). Often referred to as *paran* ("blue-green color"), the technique involved a long glass stick that was ground to a fine powder and fired to 932°F (500°C).

Beginning in the nineteenth-century Joseon dynasty, the technique began to incorporate four main colors but later developed many shades of enamel. The technique was popular in the royal court and upper classes for ceremonial decorative items such as the queen's hair ornaments. These carved-jade ornaments were decorated with multiple color enamels, gemstones, and kingfisher feather inlays, with fine-wire filigree for fluttering units via coiling wire ends added with corals, carved small butterflies, and pearls.

After the thirty-five-year-long Japanese occupation (1910–1945) and the Korean War (1950–1953), these ornaments were revived beginning in the 1970s as artists returned to the old court of Korea and started to teach techniques to women artists. *Chilbo* was revived with help from such artists as Japanese Korean princess Lee Bangja and sculptor and professor Kim Chungsook, who had studied enameling at the Cleveland Institute of Art and did her graduate studies at Cranbook Academy of Art. Furthermore, many young artists came back to Korea after studying in Japan, Germany, and America and introduced Western styles of enameling through small group workshops as well as art competitions and group exhibitions.

Korea's first enameling association was founded in 1983, and group exhibitions have been active since 1989.

Art departments at universities began to teach *chilbo* as part of their metal arts programs since the 1980s. Today many contemporary Korean enamel artists are active, offering combinations of the traditional art form and contemporary ideas and techniques.

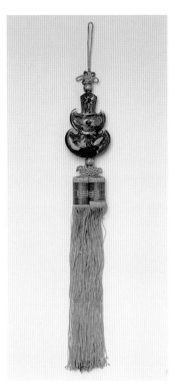

Ssang-Garakji. No. 039. Double ring sets. Joseon dynasty, 1392–1897 CE. Silver, enamel. 9.8" × 1.2". *Sookmyung Women's University Museum*

Banul-chimtong Norigae. No. 053. Needle-case pendant. Joseon dynasty, 1392–1897 CE. Silver, enamel. 12.8". *Sookmyung Women's University Museum*

Hair Ornaments. JM No. 113. Joseon dynasty, nineteenth century. Silver, amber, pearl, jade, enamel. 6" × 3" × 0.8" each. *Collection of Cheonmisa*

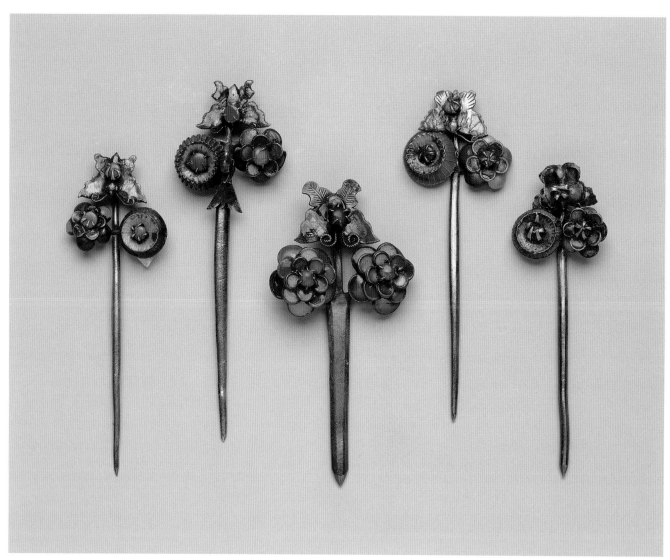

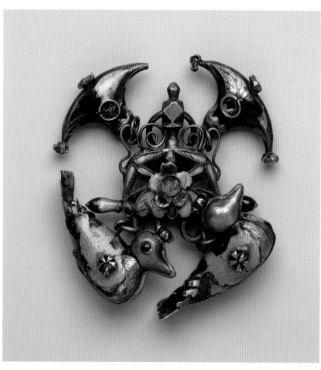

Hair Pins with Flowers & Butterfly Design. No. 018. Joseon dynasty, 1932–1910 CE. Silver, enamel. 3.0"–3.8". *Sookmyung Women's University Museum*

Norigae with Two Ducks and Two Hatchets. No. 073-2. Pendant. Joseon dynasty, 1392–1897 CE. Silver, enamels. 2.6". *Sookmyung Women's University Museum*

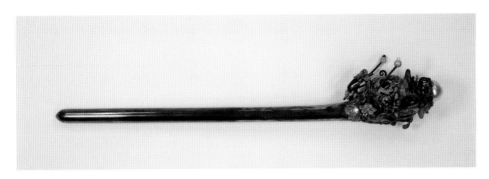

Yeongrakbong-jam Binyo. No. 2290. Hair stick. Joseon dynasty, nineteenth century. This hair stick was worn by queens, princesses, and other members of the royal household for major ceremonies. The *Yeongrak-jam* is a great work among hairpins, decorated with various gems. *Chilbo.* Silver, enamel, various gemstones. 10.2". *Seokjuseon Dankook University Museum*

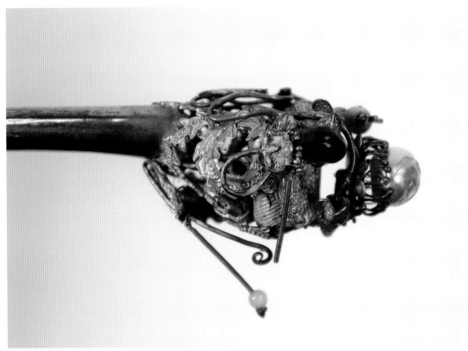

Yeongrakbong-jam Binyo. No. 2290 (close-up). *Seokjuseon Dankook University Museum*

Hair-Parting Ornamental Hairpins Twiggoji. No. 27. Joseon dynasty, nineteenth century. *Chilbo* (enameling). Silver, coral, and enamel. 2.4–3.4". Coral and enameling decorated around apricot flowers. An accessory stuck into a chignon for ornaments, used among upper-class women. *Ewha Woman's University Museum, CHANG Pudeok Memorial Gallery*

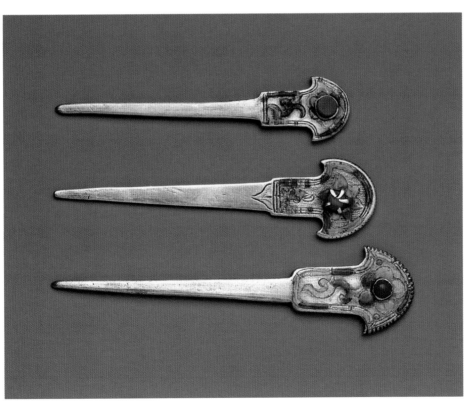

Sam-Jack Norigae. No. 2408. Three *norigae* pendants with shapes of a scarecrow, pocketknife (*jangdo*), and long-life character. Joseon dynasty, nineteenth century. The pendants shapes are a scarecrow (brings luck), pocketknife (brings protection), and character meaning long life (brings wealth and honor), and the silk tassels are in royal colors of aqua, pink, and deep purple of Korean macramé. *Chilbo, filigree,* and *jangseok.* Silver, enameling, coral. 15.7". *Seokjuseon Memorial Dankook University Museum*

Chiljack Norigae Pendant with Sevenfolds Ornaments. No. 064. Nineteenth century. Enameling (*chilbo*), *jangseok*, and hammer-chasing-engraving (*jjoi ipsa*). Silver, coral, enameling, and silk thread of Korean macramé. 17.7". *Sookmyung Women's University Museum*

Hair Ornament. JM-113. Joseon dynasty, nineteenth century. Silver, amber, pearl, jade, enamel (cloisonné). 6". *Collection of Cheonmisa*

I apply enamel to copper and stainless-steel mesh by using the wet-packing method. Low firing brings out a unique texture in the surface, and heat-treated copper mesh accentuates the texture and color of the enamel.

I produce work by using a variety of combinations of copper and stainless-steel mesh, cutting and folding seams together. I created my pieces by using the concept of Korean traditional patchwork wrapping cloth (*bojagi*) in my work. The patterns, enameled on the mesh with underfired designs, express the texture of fabric and embroidery through alternative materials and reinterpretation of the traditional patchworks in my contemporary enameling works.

Enameling (*Chilbo*) Demonstration by KO Myungjin

1. The beauty of Korean *bojagi* (traditional patchwork) wrapping cloth is inspiration for my work. Embroidery or patchwork techniques, or a combination of the two textile methods, were applied to a variety of fabrics to create characteristic textures and transparency.
2. Prepare squares from raw or heat-treated copper or brass mesh. Stainless-steel mesh is also used occasionally.
3. Use the wet-packing technique to apply lead-free enamel onto the copper mesh, according to the design.
4. After the piece is completely dry, fire in the kiln at low temperature (below 1200°F for 10 to 20 seconds) so that the surface of the fired enamel resembles the texture of embroidery (similar to the orange peel stage).
5. Pickle in the acid bath and rinse the piece well.
6. Oxidize with liver of sulfur. Apply a light coating of vegetable oil to the back side of the piece and wipe off the excess. Make sure that the holes of the mesh are not blocked. The oil prevents the color of the metal mesh from changing. When applying the oil, make sure that the oil does not touch the enameled side.
7. Following the pattern, draw a line by using a needlepoint scribe and steel ruler. Cut the pattern with shears, leaving a margin of mesh for the folded seam.
8. Fold the seams and join the pieces.
9. Assemble the remaining enameled mesh squares, using the same method.
10. The assembled pieces are firmly pinched with large, flat pliers. This effect produces a transparent quality that resembles *bojagi* made of silk voile or ramie.

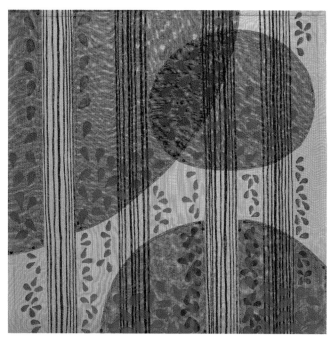

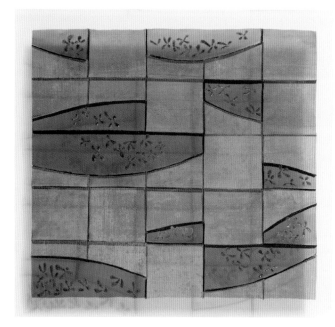

고명진 (高明辰) KO Myungjin.
Windflower. Wall relief. 2008.
Enameling on mesh, patina. Copper
mesh, fine-silver enameling. 12" ×
12" × 0.8".

고명진 (高明辰) KO Myungjin.
Remiscene 8. Wall relief. 2007.
Enameling, folding, stitching,
patina. Copper mesh, brass mesh,
enameling. 16" × 16" × 0.5".

고명진 (高明辰) KO Myungjin.
Repose-2. Wall relief. 2016.
Enameling, patina. Copper. 8.5" ×
8.5" × 0.4".

Demonstration of *Sun-Chilbo* (Cloisonné Enameling) on Moon-Shaped Bowl by KIM Miyoun (1956–2017)

1. Prepare the design and equipment.
2. Bend cloisonné wire cells according to the design.
3. Place bent cloisonné wire cells on the stainless-steel shallow plate. Anneal cloisonné wires in the kiln.
4. Dip the cloisonné wires in the CMC mixture. Place the cloisonné wire on the bowl.
5. Make twisted toilet paper bundles and cut the bundles into short blotters to soak up moisture.
6. Apply repeated shaded layers of enamel. Dry and fire.
7. Stone after last enameling and bowl before the last quick firing.
8. Finished work: *Moon-Shaped Vessel*. 14 Ga. fine silver. 9" × 7.5" × 9".

김미연 (金美延) KIM Miyoun. *Bojagii Story*. Wall relief. 2001. The design of this piece is inspired by the traditional Korean wrapping cloth *bojagi*, which is made of several patched clothes. *Chilbo*. Fine silver. 16" × 15" × 1.3".

김미연 (金美延) KIM Miyoun. *Abundance*. Vessel. 2015. An abundance of peonies traditionally means the arrival of happiness and prosperity. *Abundance* displays these flowers in fine, subtle colors. Cloisonné enameling technique (*chilbo*). Fine-silver vessel with fine-silver wire cloisonné. 6.7" × 4.7" × 2.7".

Enameling (*Chilbo*) Demonstration by BAE Changsook

1. Bisque-fire a layer of transparent white enamel onto a shallow copper bowl.
2. Transfer design pattern to enameled bowl.
3. Draw outlines of design with black enamel pencil.
4. Paint and blend with a fine-tip brush to produce the effect of a watercolor painting.
5. Dry completely before firing at 1436°F–1472°F (780°C–800°C).
6. Stone the surface with diamond-coated whetstones.
7. Paint and blend an additional layer to refine the design.
8. Dry again and refire the work.
9. Clean the edges with a green scrubber and oxidize the work in potassium sulfate.

BAE's design source.

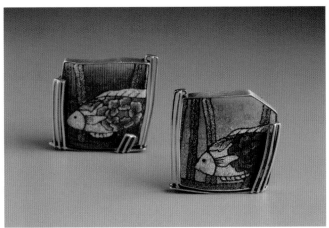

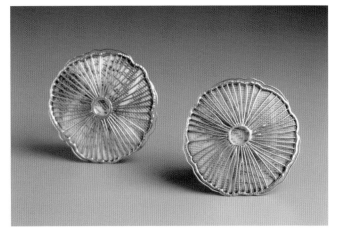

배창숙 (裵昌淑) BAE
Changsook. *Bring Flowers Rainy
Day*. Plate. 2014. Wet-packing
enameling (*chilbo*). Copper and
enamel. 2" × 10" × 10".

배창숙 (裵昌淑) BAE
Changsook. *Strolling*. Brooches.
2014. Enameling (*chilbo*). Copper,
sterling silver, enamel, lusters.
2.28" × 2.2" × 0.48" each.

배창숙 (裵昌淑) BAE
Changsook. *Long Walk*. Brooches.
2014. Enameling (*chilbo*).
Copper, sterling silver, enamel.
3" × 2.92" × 0.28" each.

HONG Kyung Hee

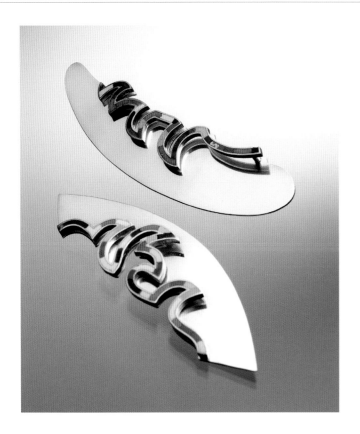

홍경희 (洪京姬) HONG Kyung Hee. *Shape of Colors*. Brooches. 2010. Forming, fabricating, enameling, and assembling with cold joining. Fine and sterling silver, copper, enameling (*chilbo*). 3.68" × 1.72" × 0.48" each.

CHOO Won Gyo

추원교 (秋園敎) CHOO Won Gyo. *Anxiously Waiting to See Him at the Airport Gate . . .* Wall relief. 2008. Enameling (*chilbo*) drawing, wet-packing methods. Copper, duralumin, enamel, and mother-of-pearl. 22.8" × 31.6" × 1".

장애지 (張愛志) JANG Aeji. *A Story of Lotus Flower V & VI.* Korean-style pendant (*norigae*). 2015. Wet packing and cloisonné (*yuson chilbo*). Fine-silver cloisonné wire, sterling silver, enamel, hand-dyed silk thread macramé and tassels. 2" × 2" × 0.4"; 18".

Lotus flowers are popular in traditional Korean art. The lotus flowers symbolize innocence and wishes to flourish in wealth and children bearing, especially boys. Jang's pendants are crafted with handmade silk threads and macramé tassels (*norigae*). These are worn on a traditional Korean woman's outfit between the top and skirt (*jeogori* and *chima*). They are especially used for Korean-style wedding rituals and are usually worn on special occasions among married women with Korean outfits.

My work is an attempt to visualize spiritually important elements of my life through various physical materials such as silver, stained glass, and enamels. Shelters such as houses are a frequent design element in my pieces. I also use the imagery of fish both as a Christian symbol for new life and as a symbol of life-giving water.

These elements are executed on a plane surface. I strengthen their effect and form by adding geometric shapes, usually hexagons, to create emotional impact.

Enameling on Glass Demonstration by JANG Mee Yeon

This enameling-on-stained-glass technique was developed through trial and error, since it is quite different from the regular enameling process. This technique is similar to glazing ceramic works.

1. After applying enamel to the glass, the piece is put into a cold kiln, which is set for 1,472°F.
2. When the temperature reaches 1,472°F, the kiln is turned off and the piece is allowed to cool completely before removing from the kiln. This firing is repeated as many times as necessary until all desired colors are applied.
3. Each enamel layer must be very thin, since a thick layer may cause the piece to break because of an unbalanced coefficient of expansion across the glass surface.

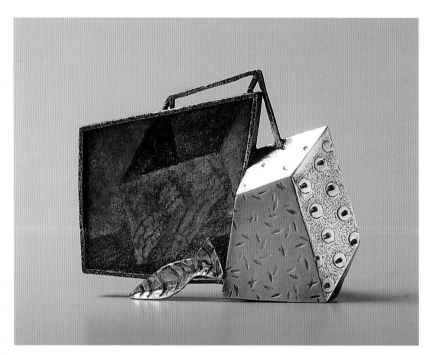

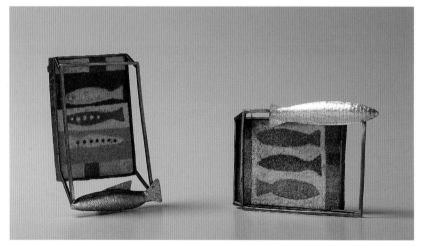

장미연 (張美燕) JANG Mee Yeon. *Shelter 96.* Brooch. 1996. Roll-printing texturing, forming, constructing, fabricated, *keum-boo* application, oxidizing, and assembling 3-D sculptural brooch. Sterling silver, enamel on copper, 24K gold overlay. 2" × 2.8" × 0.6".

장미연 (張美燕) JANG Mee Yeon. *Shelter 97.* Brooches. 1997. Roller printing, forming, fabricating, setting, 24K gold overlaying (*keum-boo*), and oxidizing finish. Sterling silver, enamel on copper, 24K gold foil. 2.8" × 1.9" × 0.6"; 2" × 3" × 0.6".

장미연 (張美燕) JANG Mee Yeon.
Shelter 99. Brooch. 1999.
Enameling on glass, roller printing,
forming, constructing, *keum-boo*,
and oxidizing finish. Sterling silver,
enamel on glass, 24K gold foil.
1.7" × 2.3" × 0.4".

정복희 (鄭福姬) JUNG Bokhee.
Sweet Seventeen. Coffee set. 2006.
Raising, texturing, fabricating,
enameling, stone setting, and
finishing. Fine silver, cloisonné
enameling (*seon chilbo*), lapis
lazuli. 4.7" × 3.15" × 3.15"; 4.7"
× 5.5" × 3.15"; 7" × 6.7" × 4".
    This coffee set was created to
celebrate a girl's seventeenth
birthday. The set is decorated with
enameled delicate blue flowers.

Enameling on Electroformed Brooches and Applied *Ottchil* by KIM Heejoo

The process of adding metal layers on the carved-wax object in an electroforming bath represents the creation of new life. Several layers of light-sifted enameling help enhance the electroformed structure and achieve natural soft colors.

The several layers of applied *ottchil* (Korean lacquer) colors also represent the accumulation of time. *Ottchil* is a traditional Korean traditional technique that is used to protect surfaces vulnerable to external stimulus. Through this process, the works are born with a powerful vitality that extends beyond the flow of time.

김희주 (金希柱) KIM Heejoo.
Fifth Season I. Neck piece. 2010.
Electroforming, enameling
(*chilbo*). Wax, copper, leather,
thread. 5.7" × 4.2" × 3.2".

김희주 (金希柱) KIM Heejoo.
Fifth Season III. Brooch. 2012.
Electroforming, enameling (*chilbo*).
Wax, copper, Korean traditional oil
paper, enamel. 4.3" × 3.2" × 1.8".

The artist uses an enameling process that mimics the delicacy of drawing and oriental brush painting. She creates images of quietly flowing and harmoniously changing landscapes as seen through the flow of time. Her enameling technique involves first making a form as if drawing a picture with a pencil, then covering the form with enameling and firing the piece several times at 1382°F (750°C).

문선영 (文善暎) MOON Sunyoung. *Peace*. Wall hanging. 2016. *Chilbo*. Copper, fine silver, enameling pencil, enamel. 6" × 6" × 0.8".

Peace evokes the likeness of a pencil rendering of an oriental painting.

KOREAN TRADITIONAL *CHILBO* (ENAMELING)
SKILLS TRANSMITTER, DESIGNATED BY THE
MINISTRY OF LABOR, 2012–2014.

NOH Yongsook produces and conducts
educational demonstrations for children
and adults, as well as producing items
for tourists.

노용숙 (盧鏞淑) NOH Yongsook.
Saekdong. Food container. 1995.
Constructed, fabricated, enameling (*chilbo*). Silver enamel.
2" × 9.4" × 9.4".

노용숙 (盧鏞淑) NOH Yongsook.
A Couple of Lovebirds. Object. 2013.
Fine silver, enamel (*chilbo*). Silver,
enamel. 2" × 2.2" × 0.4" each.

China Painting Work Process

The brooch was electroformed and enameled at a high temperature, 1472°F–1652°F (800°C–900°C).

After cooling completely, the brooch is partially painted with China painting and then left to dry out. Finally the piece is fired at a low temperature 329°F (165°C) for 45 minutes to highlight colored areas.

After finishing brooches, colored areas are painted with China painting. They are completely dried and fired at a low temperature of 329°F (165°C) for 45 minutes.

박은주 (朴恩珠) PARK Eunju. *Fill 2*. Brooch. 2008. China painting. Silver. 4.13" × 1.8" × 1.7".

박은주 (朴恩珠) PARK Eunju. *Tilt*. Necklace. 2008. China painting. Silver, silk thread, enamel. 24" × 1.2" × 12".

박미향 (朴美香) PARK Mihyang. *Painting of Joseon Dynasty Bookshelves.* Wall plaque. 2012. *Chilbo.* Copper, fine-silver wire, enameling, silver paper. 13.2" × 8.8" × 0.36".

During the Joseon dynasty, fourteenth–nineteenth centuries, it was popular to hang wall paintings of books and flowers (folk paintings) in noble men's study rooms to encourage children to study.

박미향 (朴美香) PARK Mihyang. *Flower & Calligraphy.* Wall plaque. 2016. *Chilbo.* Copper, fine-silver wire, enameling, silver paper. 8.8" × 6" × 0.36".

This represents the wall paintings depicting flowers and ancient Chinese calligraphy that were very popular during the Joseon dynasty.

박미향 (朴美香) PARK Mihyang. *The Wedding Day.* Wedding crown (*jokduri*) and hair sticks. 2012. *Chilbo.* Fine silver, enameling. 5.6" × 4.4" × 6".

Jokduri is a head ornament of queens and noble women that was worn on their wedding day or during important ceremonies during the Joseon dynasty, ninth century.

YOON Jungwha

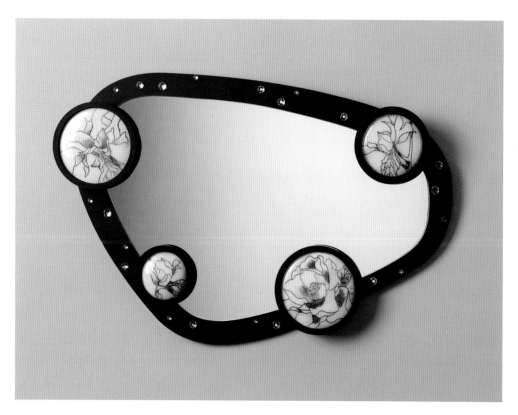

윤정화 (尹正和) YOON Jungwha. *Spring 1, Mirror 1.* 2016. *Sgraffito* enameling. Enamel, acrylic, Swarovski crystal, mirror. 9.2" × 14" × 2".

    This mirror is created with circular enameling, showing the spring, and is done with *sgraffito* enameling technique, and crystals are used on the black-colored acrylic band.

YUN Juyeon

윤주연 (尹姝然) YUN Juyeon. *For You II.* Brooch. 2014. Forming, assembling, fabricating, enameling (*chilbo*), oxidizing, and enameling pencil drawing. Copper, fine-silver foil, sterling silver, enamel, enameling pencil. 6.4" × 2" × 1.4".

윤주연 (尹姝然) YUN Juyeon. *Restful I.* Brooch. 2015. Forming, assembling, fabricating, enameling (*chilbo*), oxidizing, and enameling pencil drawing. Copper, fine-silver foil, enamel, enameling pencil, wood. 11" × 4" × 2.8"; 9.2" × 3.4" × 3".

    Yun Juyeon's enamel works utilize underglazed pencil and fine-silver foil. They show her concern for keeping special feelings, such as looking at fresh flowers. She wishes that those who look at her enameled flowers keep and maintain feelings similar to those one gets from fresh flowers.

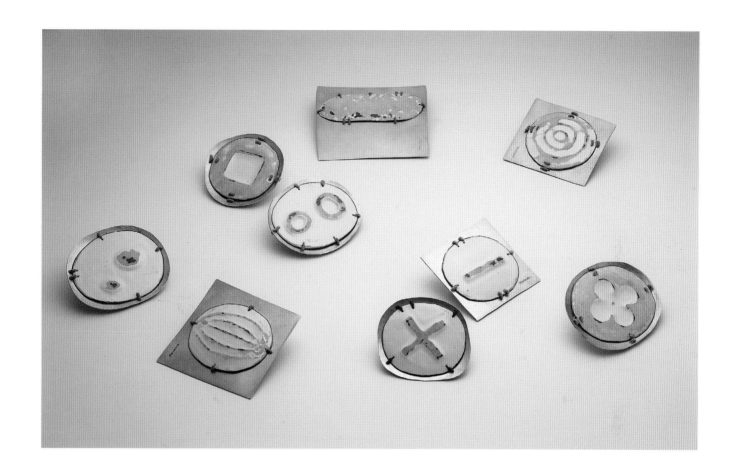

류연희(柳延熹) RYU Yeunhee.
Winter Brooches. Installation. 2010.
Created with simple techniques of
chasing and repoussé (*tachul*) on
silver. Edges of the spoons are
punch-stitched with silver
threadlike thin wires, riveted, and
soldered. The white-enameled
(*chilbo*) surface represents winter
snow scenes. Silver and enameling. 3.3" × 3.3" × 0.5" each.

Stone-Crushed Cold Inlay
(*Dohl Seokhwe Ipsa*)

Doh seokhwe ipsa uses a process similar to cold enameling. Fine and precious stones or bricks are crushed into coarse or fine powders that are inlaid into metal to give color, texture, and a sculptural appearance. Coarse metal filings and small metal shapes are also used.

Traditionally employed by *jangseok* (traditional furniture joinery) makers, this technique has been used for furniture, locks, and metal money (as seen below).

Today, some artists use these methods for inlay work to include special colors and forms in their large-scale sculptural forms, and within small sections of their jewelry work.

Historical References: Museum Collections

Dowry Key Charm. Late Joseon dynasty, nineteenth century. No. 20071104/002330. Brass, stone powder (*dohl ipsa*) with mineral dye, iron, and silk tassel. 12" × 6" × 0.8". *Dohl seokchae ipsa. Collection of Lock Museum*

Dowry Key 3 Charms. Late *Joseon* dynasty, nineteenth century. No. 200711/00230. Brass, stone powder (*dohl ipsa*) with mineral dye, iron, silk, and silk tassel. 6" × 2" x 0.8". *Dohl seokchae ipsa. Collection of Lock Museum*

Demonstration of Stone-Crushed Cold Inlay (*Dohl Seokhwe Ipsa*) by KANG Chan Kyun

1. Use sinking and raising to make two shallow 24" (60 cm) diameter bowls from 12-gauge (2 mm thick) copper. Braze (or weld) the two shallow bowls together to create the face.
2. Roughly grind both sides of the face with #80 disk grinder to prepare the surface to accept the mixture of Polycoat. Pound chips of different-colored bricks with a long-handled hammer to create rough powder.
3. Solder metal tubing for the mustache and eyes with lead solder. Grind off the top of the tubing to show 3-D appearances.
4. Mix copper dust with Polycoat and spread over the middle of the mustache and nose area. Let dry about one hour.
5. Mix brass powder made from band saw waste with Polycoat and spread over the forehead area.
6. Mix with powder and spread over designated area of tiger's face.
7. Grind with disc grinder and water.
8. Grind with hand piece (flexible shaft) with an assortment of grinding bits for creating textures.

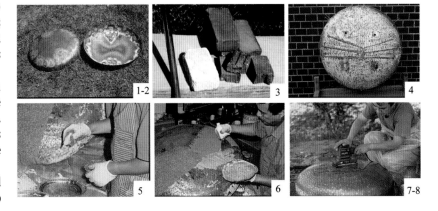

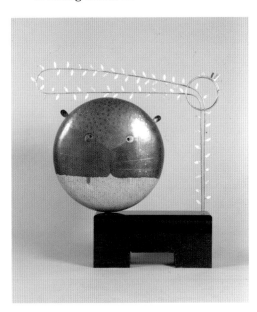

강찬균 (姜燦均) KANG Chan Kyun, member of the National Academy of the Arts (in Fine Metal Arts) of the Republic of Korea. *Tiger & Hoop* (completed demonstration piece). Object. 1989. Stone particle inlay (*seokhwei* inlay). Copper, brass, 18K gold, silver, granite. 55.2" × 52" × 12". *Collection of Korean National Museum of Modern & Contemporary Art*

KANG Chan Kyun

MEMBER OF THE NATIONAL ACADEMY OF THE
REPUBLIC OF KOREA IN FINE METAL ARTS.
SELECTED AND APPOINTED BY THE NATIONAL
ACADEMY OF THE ARTS

강찬균 (姜燦均) KANG Chan
Kyun, member of the National
Academy of the Arts (in Fine Metal
Arts) of the Republic of Korea. *Baby
Tiger*. Object. 2003. Crushed-stone
inlay (*seokhwei ipsa*). Copper,
nickel silver, brass, stone particles.
17.5" × 22" × 10".

강찬균 (姜燦均) KANG Chan Kyun, member of the National Academy of the Arts (in Fine Metal Arts) of the Republic of Korea. *Pink Persimmon Hongsi*. Object. 1999. Crushed-stone inlay (*seokhwei ipsa*). Copper, brass, nickel silver, stone particles, marble. 22" × 18" × 8".

CHOO Yaekyung

주예경 (周禮敬) CHOO Yaekyung. *Longing*. Brooch. 2007. Chasing and repoussé, fabrication, carving, and mineral color powder with animal glue painting, *tachul*, and stone powder (*dohl ipsa*) painting. Sterling silver, copper, mineral color powder on wood, animal glue. 3.1" × 2" × 7.9".

CHAPTER 7

Jade-Carving Techniques

Traditional Korean jade carvings were not as elaborate as Chinese carvings, but jade ornaments retain historical importance for their role in royal courts beginning in the Neolithic period. These ornaments were mainly kings' ear ornaments and crowns, decorated with small peanut-shaped pieces of jade called *gogok*.

Jade was actively used during the Joseon dynasty (nineteenth century), a golden age for Korea's jade work. Craftsmen formed Buddhist motifs, cicadas, and peanut-shaped good-luck talismans on small- and large-scale architectural pieces. The queen and upper-class women of the royal courts wore hair ornaments and rings embellished with decorative metal designs. These designs were decorated with wire-coiled fluttering units, coral, and jade beads.

The contemporary use of jade can be seen in carved ornaments that decorate the *norigae*, a pendant with silk tassels and large, carved double rings used on traditional Korean upper garments.

There are two universities in Korea offering majors in jade carving in their fine-crafts departments: Kyonggi University in Kyonggi City, Wonkwang University in Iksan City, and the Korean National University of Cultural Heritage in Buyeo County.

Contemporary artists add these jade embellishments to their ornamental works, especially works specifically for engagements, weddings, and important birthday celebrations, as jade brings good health and prosperity.

Necklace. NT No. 634. Silla
dynasty, fifth–sixth centuries. Glass
and jade. 6.3". *National Museum
of Korea*

Samjak Norigae. Three-part
Pendant. Joseon dynasty,
nineteenth century. Jade, coral,
amber, pearl. 57.5". *National
Palace Museum of Korea*

*Gold Necklace with Jade Gogok
Pendant.* NT No. 456. Silla dynasty,
early sixth century. 32.7". *National
Museum of Korea*

Hair Ornament Pin. No. 126. Joseon dynasty, nineteenth century. Queen's white-jade, long hair stick. White jade, pearl, coral, kingfisher feather (*bichimo*). 7.5". *National Palace Museum of Korea*

Hair Ornament Pin. No. 126 (close-up).

Queen's White Jade Long Hairpin: Jewelry Ornament. No. 129. Joseon dynasty, nineteenth century. Jade carving, granulation, filigree construction. Carved jade, silver, pearl, coral, and red and blue glass (*hongparii, chongparii*), kingfisher feather overlay glued with fish gluten glue set in frames set on the carved phoenix, with movable wrapping-wire tips and pearls riveted by coral beads. 9.96". *National Palace Museum of Korea*

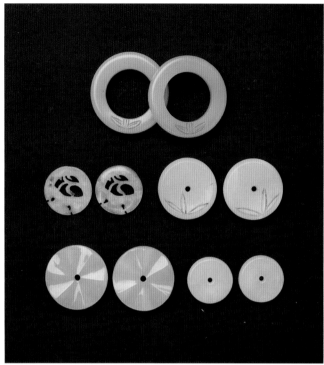

King's Crown. NT No. 191. Silla
dynasty, fifth century. Gold, jade.
10.9". *Gyeongju National Museum*

Ghwancha. Men's head ornaments.
Nos. 091–092. Joseon dynasty,
1392–1897 CE. Jade and agate.
0.6" × 1.4". *Sookmyung Women's
University Museum*

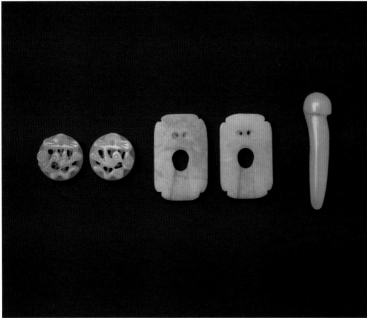

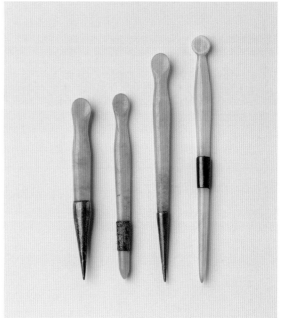

Danchu. No. 084. Buttons made of amber. Joseon dynasty, nineteenth century. 0.8"–1.1". *Sookmyung Women's University Museum*

Donggot and Ghwancha. No. 089. Joseon dynasty, 1392–1897 CE. Ornamental hairpins and ornaments for men. Coral, jade, agate, and silver. Joseon dynasty, 1392–1897 CE. 1.48"–1.8". *Sookmyung Women's University Museum*

Ghwancha. Nos. 089, 091. Joseon dynasty, 1392–1897 CE. Hair ornaments for men. Jade. 0.6" × 1.4". *Sookmyung Women's University Museum*

Hairpins with Ear-Pick Designs. No. 023. Joseon dynasty, 1392–1897 CE. Silver, jade. 2.6"–3.7". *Sookmyung Women's University Museum*

KIM Young Hee

GYEONGGI-DO INTANGIBLE CULTURAL ASSET NO.
18: OK-JANG (JADE CRAFTSPERSON) JEWELRY
MASTER AND PRACTITIONER

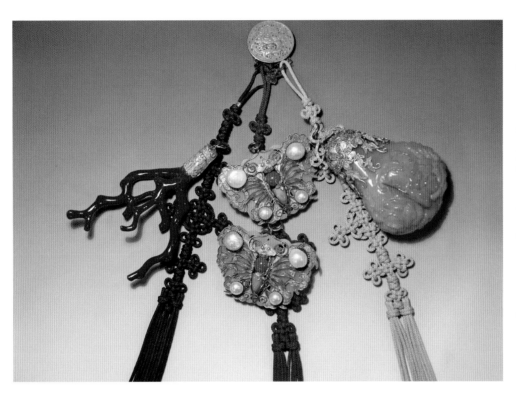

김영희 (金泳熙) KIM Young Hee,
Gyeonggi-do Intangible Cultural Asset
No. 18: Ok-Jang (Jade Craftsperson)
Jewelry Master and Practitioner.
King Youngchin and Queen
Young's Large Samjak Norigae
Replica. Three-section-long
pendant with tassels. 1996. Jade
carving, metal constructing, and
joinery. White and pink jade, 24K
gold, silver, coral, amber, pearls,
turquoise, and kingfisher feather
inlay (paran bichimo). 20".
Samjak Norigae is a large,
three-part traditional Korean
pendant, with three separate
themes on each unit: coral
branches, a pair of butterflies, and
carved amber. The red-coral
branches have two important
symbolic meanings; the color red
prevents bad luck in shamanistic
tradition, and the coral branches
stretched out in many directions
symbolize prosperity of descen-
dants. The amber is sculpted in the
shape of a fingered citron, which
looks like the hand of Buddha.
Peonies and bats are carved into
the surface, with peonies
representing wealth and honor,
and bats representing good
fortune. The pair of butterflies in
the middle represents happiness.
They are crafted from pearls, coral,
and malachite. These grand and
splendid ornaments are identical
to the ones used by King
Youngchin's queen, Queen Young,
during ceremonial royal-court
rituals. Collection of Baekbong
Korean Traditional Jewelry &
Ornament Museum

김영희, 金泳熙 KIM Young Hee
Replica Jade Ornament of King
Youngchin Waist Ornament, 2003.
Jade, brass, silk. 47" × 1.7 " (118 ×
4.3 cm). Jade carving, metal joinery,
and silk laminating. Collection of
Baekbong Korean Traditional Jewelry
& Ornament Museum

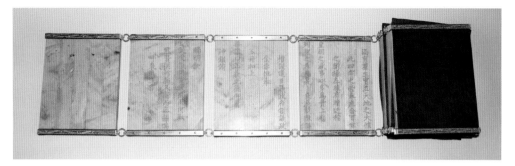

김영희 金泳熙 KIM Young Hee
Jade Book with Royal Writings, 2006.
Jade, 24K gold, yellow brass, silk. 8.7"
× 6.3" (22 × 16 cm). Jade carving,
24K gold writing with *keumpak*
technique, and joinery. *Collection of
Baekbong Korean Traditional Jewelry
& Ornament Museum*

Jade Flower & Butterfly Fluttering Hair Stick Pins Demonstration by KIM Young Hee

1. Slice jade on the diamond cutter.
2. Cut jade according to the design.
3. Drill holes for the units to be set.
4. Finish base jade plate and polish the foundation plate.
5. Construct each setting in silver.
6. Examine each setting to ensure they fit the stones.
7. After making the final fitted settings, plate all units to 24K gold.
8. Glue Kingfisher feathers to the setting and secure all gems into the settings.
9. Apply flattering settings of pearls and other gems to the butterfly hair ornaments.
10. Completed hair ornaments.

김영희 (金泳熙) KIM Young Hee,
Gyeonggi-do Intangible Cultural
Asset No. 18: *Ok-Jang* (Jade
Craftsperson) Jewelry Master and
Practitioner. *Three White Jade
Hair Ornaments, Replica of
19th-Century Queen's Hair
Stick-Pin Ornaments.* Hair pin
ornaments. 2000. 24" × 20" × 20"
each. All twisted wires tremble as
the wearer is marching in the
procession; national wedding
ceremonies use these types of
ornaments. Carved white jade,
silver, 24K gold wire, setting with
red and blue glasses (*hongparii*
and *chongparii*), pearls, kingfisher feather glued with hide
glue in the frames, enameling,
and filigree. *Collection of
Baekbong Korean Traditional
Jewelry & Ornament Museum*

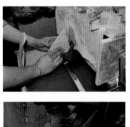
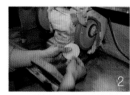

Demonstration of Serpentine Jade Carving Process by JANG Seok

Flower-Carving Process

1. Design the flower pattern
2. Trace design onto the serpentine jade
3. Begin shaping the flower with a diamond cutter
4. Define the shape
5. Grind the entire surface
6. Finish jade carving
7. Sand with wet-stone
8. Sand with sandpaper
9. Polish the flower

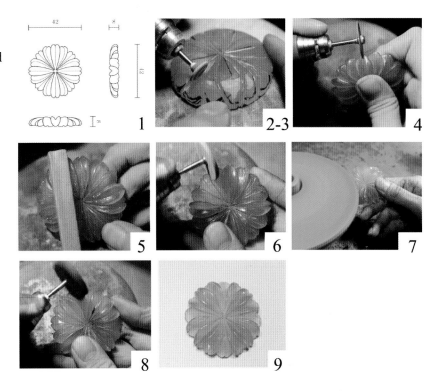

Butterfly-Carving Process

1. Design the butterfly pattern
2. Trace design onto the serpentine jade
3. Cut out the shape using the diamond cutter
4. Define the shape
5. Grind the entire surface and finish carving
6. As with flower project, sand with wet-stone, sandpaper, and then polish

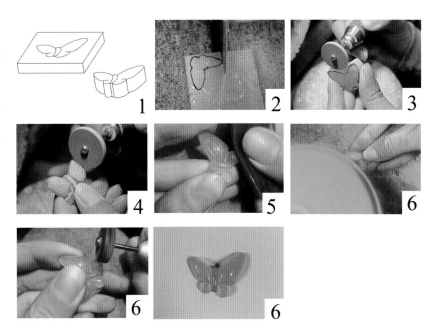

JANG Seok

DESIGNATED ASSISTANT INSTRUCTOR FOR
SUCCESSOR TRAINING OF THE NATIONAL
INTANGIBLE CULTURAL HERITAGE NO. 100:
OK-JANG (JADE CRAFTSPERSON)

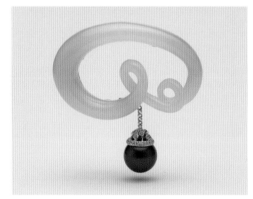

장석 (張錫) JANG Seok, Jade Crafts Designated Assistant No. 100: *Ok-Jang* (Jade Craftsperson) Jewelry Master and Practitioner. *Dragons & Clouds*. Teapot and cup. 2016. Carving and inlay (*ok* hammer-chisel and 24K gold powder *ipsa*). Nephrite jade, 24K gold powder. 7" × 4" × 3.6"; 2.6" × 1.6" × 1.6".

장석 (張錫) JANG Seok, Jade Crafts Designated Assistant No. 100: *Ok-Jang* (Jade Craftsperson) Jewelry Master and Practitioner. *Dragons & Clouds* (close-up).

장석 (張錫) JANG Seok, Jade Crafts Designated Assistant No. 100: *Ok-Jang* (Jade Craftsperson) Jewelry Master and Practitioner. *Melody of Jade V*. Necklace and earrings set. 2008. Jade (*ok*) carving. Jade, 14K white gold, topaz.

장석 (張錫) JANG Seok, Jade Crafts Designated Assistant No. 100: *Ok-Jang* (Jade Craftsperson) Jewelry Master and Practitioner. *Melody of Jade VI*. Brooch. 2008. Jade (*ok*) carving. Jade, 14K white gold, black pearl. 2.4" × 2.2" × 0.8".

AN Jung Hee

안정희 (安正熙) AN Jung Hee. *Relationship.* Necklace. 2007. Jade (*ok*) carving. Jade, sterling silver, and chain. 2.8" × 2.4" × 0.4"; 22".

CHOI Yangsun

최양선 (崔良先) CHOI Yangsun. *Chalice Ciborium Paten.* Bowl. 2014. Spun raising, forming, planishing, gold plaiting, jade carving, fabricating, assemble setting, rivet finishing. Jade, sterling silver, gold-plated chalice inside. 8.8 × 2.8" × 2.8"; 3.6" × 5.2" × 5.2"; 0.8" × 3.2" × 3.2".

PARK Young Seon

박영선 (朴榮善) PARK Young Seon.
Cactus. Brooch. 2011. Jade (*ok*)
carving. Jade, sterling silver, agate,
amber, coral. 5.9" × 5.9" × 0.5" each.

SHIN Eun Joo

신은주 (申恩珠) SHIN Eun Joo.
Spoon & Chopstick Rests. Three
sets of rests. 2007. Jade (*ok*)
carving. Sterling silver, jade, coral,
mother-of-pearl. 2" × 2" × 0.8".

CHAPTER 8

Metalcraft for Wedding Rituals, Ornaments, and Gift Exchange Ceremony (*Hollye* and *Yemul*)

The traditional Korean marriage ceremony (*hollye-sik*) is a Confucian ceremony. During the ceremony, water basins made of brass and Korean wine sets made of silver, brass, or ceramic were used.

The bride would wear a wedding hairdo with a *jokduri* (wedding crown with special hair piece) decorated with jade, amber, coral, pearls, or beads with gold or silver wire-wrapping/connecting ends (riveted), which moved as the bride walked.

Before the ceremony, it was common for the bride to send gifts of silverware, spoon and chopstick sets (*sujeo*), and Korean dresses or garments. These gifts, called *yemul*, usually included two sets of rice bowls, soup bowls with lids, and two sets of spoons and chopsticks. Special containers were added, such as candy/fruit containers or *goo-joul-pan*, a nine-sectioned, eight-sided container with a lid.

The groom's home in turn would gift the bride with several traditional ornaments, such as 24K gold, silver, jade, or gold double rings with special symbolic designs and gold ornaments, and other traditional outfits and gift items.

The bride prepared special furniture such as ornate chests of drawers and a personal makeup stand decorated with *ottchil* and mother-of-pearl overlay to bring to her new home.

In a traditional wedding, the groom would arrive at the bride's house three days before the wedding, accompanied by a wedding chest (*ham*) containing the legal certificate of his family tree document, sealed in an envelope by the chest bearer (*hamjinaebi*) and a wedding master (*honju*).

Korean weddings today usually include parts of these traditions. After the Western-style ceremony, there is often a traditional Korean wedding ceremony (*paebaek*) where the bride wears a traditional wedding dress, wedding crown with hair piece (*jokduri*), and a long hair stick (*binyeo*). The bride will perform the traditional bow with two wedding coordinators' support—one at each arm to support her during the deep and long bow—for the traditional formal rite of *paebaek*, where she greets her parents-in-law and receives their special blessings, such as a happy, healthy, and long marriage with her new husband (*sillang*) and bearing many children, especially sons.

Koreans are unique among Asian cultures in that they use both spoons and chopsticks as eating utensils. These are produced as a set (*sujeo*) traditionally made of brass and silver. As mentioned above, they also served as part of the traditional wedding gifts.

From the twelfth century until the Korean War, in the 1950s, brassware (an alloy of 78% copper and 22% tin) utensil sets were used among commoners. Silverware was introduced during the Goryeo dynasty (918–1392 CE) and reserved for use among upper classes for special occasions and for guests. Traditionally, silver utensils were used by the royal family for detecting poisoned food, because the color of the utensils turns darker when it touches poison. Brass wares with large wooden serving stands with footed bases, as well as brass bowls and serving trays with footed bases, were for ceremonial use or funerary functions.

During the Korean War, the government collected the metal utensils and wares for the war effort. Since then, stainless steel and wood have been used for making eating utensils. Traditionally, wooden utensils and bowls are used in Buddhist temples.

In the early Goryeo dynasty (918–1392 CE), the spoon handle was long and curved, but in the middle period, the end of the spoon handle became split like a swallow's tail and less curved. During the later part of the Goryeo dynasty, the spoon handle became longer, straighter, and thicker, while the spoon's bowl became rounder and thinner.

Contemporary spoons usually have decorations such as 24K gold *keum-boo* letters, with designs of blessings, long lives, or special letters. The end of the handle is often inlaid with enameled flower designs or 24K gold *keum-boo* decorations.

It is customary to give these sets as gifts or use silver utensils during wedding rituals and other important events, such as a child's first birthday. Parents and grandparents have their own set of spoons and chopsticks. When an ancestor's memorial service is held, only brass utensils, bowls, and drinking cups are used. This is so that the sound of chopsticks striking the bowl acts as an invitation for the spirits to come to the service.

Spoon. No. 56.880. Goryeo dynasty, twelfth–thirteenth centuries. Bronze. *Photograph © 2018 Museum of Fine Arts, Boston*

Chopsticks. No. 17.830.1-2. Goryeo dynasty, twelfth–thirteenth centuries. Silver with engraved decoration. 10". *Photograph © 2018 Museum of Fine Arts, Boston*

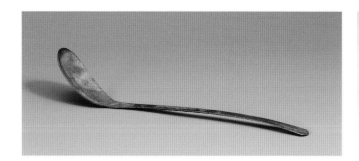

Spoon. Bon013563. Goryeo dynasty, twelfth–thirteenth centuries. Brass. 10.2". *National Museum of Korea*

Spoon. TE820. Goryeo dynasty, twelfth–thirteenth centuries. 1.1" × 3.9". *Tokyo National Museum, Japan*

Spoon. Duk003137. United Silla dynasty, ninth–tenth centuries. 11.3". *National Museum of Korea*

Various hammered *sujeo* (spoon and chopsticks sets). Ninth–twentieth centuries. 8.5"–11.3".
Collection of Lee Bongju Museum

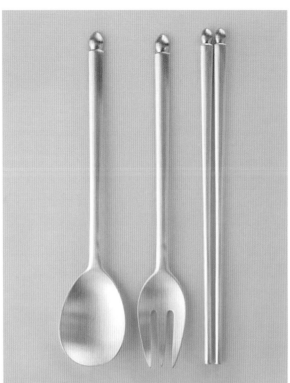

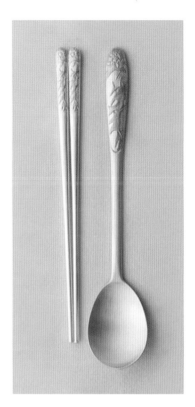

대영공방 (大榮工房) Daeyoung
Metalcrafts. *Peach.* Spoon and
chopsticks set. 2016. Forming and
press design, *keum-boo.* Sterling
silver, 24K gold foil. 8.5".

대영공방 (大榮工房) Daeyoung
Metalcrafts. *Child Set.* Spoon, fork,
and chopsticks. 2016. Forming and
press design, *keum-boo.* Sterling
silver, 24K gold foil. 6.4" each.

대영공방 (大榮工房) Daeyoung
Metalcrafts. *Lychnis.* Spoon and
chopsticks set. 2016. *Keum-boo.*
Sterling silver. 8.5"; 8.9".

김영희 (金泳熙) KIM Young Hee, *Gyeonggi-do* Intangible Cultural Asset No.18: *Ok-Jang* (Jade Craftsperson) Jewelry Master and Practitioner. *Daesumeori: Large Hair Ceremonial Wig*. Ritual hair ornament. 1995. Jade carving, metal ornament constructing, enameling, and stone setting. Jade, 24K gold, silver, pearl, enamel, red glass, blue glass, hair. 24" × 20" × 20". Museum replica. *Collection of Baekbong Korean Traditional Jewelry & Ornament Museum*

This is a replica of one of the wigs used by the queen when she was attending ceremonial rituals in the court during the Joseon dynasty. It is decorated with ornaments made of precious materials such as gold, silver, jade, and pearl. The designs contain about fourteen kinds of dragons, phoenixes, butterflies, and lotus flowers popular among the royal family.

Norigae. Pendant with butterfly-shaped ornament for *yemul.* Wedding ornament. Twentieth century. Filigree, Korean macramé. Gold, enamel, silk tassel. 2" × 11.2". *Collection of Saekdong Museum*

Bridal Wedding Knife Ornament. JM231. Joseon dynasty, nineteenth century. *Jangseok.* Silver, painting on the back of ox bone. 4". *Collection of Cheonmisa*

Bride (wearing *jokduri* and *binyeo*) and groom. Wedding ceremony. *Collection of the Saekdong Museum*

천미사 Cheonmisa Metalcrafts. *Wedding Crown and 2 Larger Hair Sticks.* Hair ornament. 2015. Lavender jade, coral, amethyst, 18K white gold. 9" each.

천미사 Cheonmisa Metalcrafts. *Wedding Hair Pin.* Wedding hair ornament. 2015. 18K gold, fine and sterling silver, enamel, amethyst, coral. 12" each.

장석 (張錫) JANG Seok, Jade
Crafts Designated Assistant No. 100:
Ok-Jang (Jade Craftsperson)
Jewelry Master and Practitioner.
Ten-Living-Beings Norigae. Wedding
perfume bottle / pendant. 2013.
Jade carving. Jade, silk thread,
Korean macramé. 10" × 2" × 1".

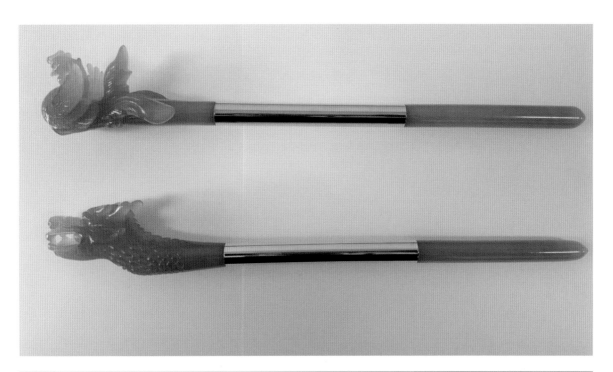

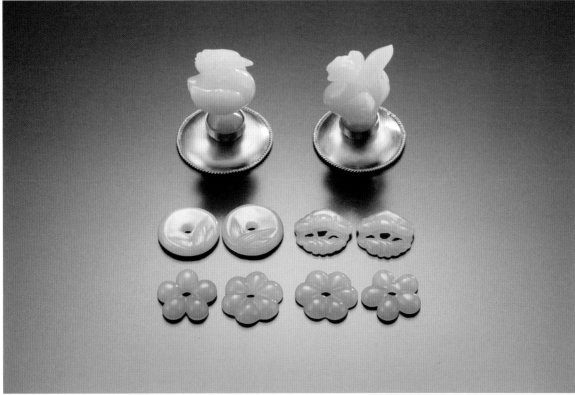

장석 (張錫) JANG Seok, Jade
Crafts Designated Assistant No.
100: *Ok-Jang* (Jade Craftsperson)
Jewelry Master and Practitioner.
*Wedding Ritual with Phoenix and
Dragon Design.* Yellow-jade back
hair pin. 2016. Jade carving, 24K
gold plated. Jade, silver. 2.5" ×
12" × 2.5"; 2" × 12" × 2".

장석 (張錫) JANG Seok, Jade
Crafts Designated Assistant No.
100: *Ok-Jang* (Jade Craftsperson)
Jewelry Master and Practitioner.
Man's Head and Button Ornaments.
Wedding ornaments. 2012. Jade
carving, 24K gold plated. Jade,
silver. 2.4" × 2" × 2"; 0.4" × 1.5"
× 1.5" each.

신라 명보랑 (新羅 明寶廊)
Shilla MyungBoRang Metalcrafts.
Twin Cranes. Nine-section food
container. 1980. Constructing,
fabricating, enameling for the
wedding ritual (*yemul*). Fine and
sterling silver, enamel. 2" × 8.8" ×
8.8". *Collection of Shilla
MyungBoRang Silver Crafts*

  Shilla MyungBoRang Metalcrafts
is a high-end shop and metal art
gallery. The shop produces and
special household and wedding
ritual ceremonies and gift
exchanges (*yemul*).

신라 명보랑 (新羅 明寶廊)
Shilla MyungBoRang Metalcrafts.
Jade Knob. Vessel with lid. 2007.
Raising, texturing, constructing,
and setting for bowl. Fine and
sterling silver, jade. 5.2" × 5" × 5".
*Collection of Shilla MyungBoRang
Silver Crafts*

신라 명보랑 (新羅 明寶廊)
Shilla MyungBoRang Metalcrafts.
Peach Pattern Knob. Vessel with
lid. 1983. Raising, forming,
texturing, cloisonné enameling
(*yuseon chilbo*), assembling, and
setting for wedding ritual (*yemul*).
Fine and sterling silver, enamel.
5.2" × 2.8" × 2.8". *Collection of
Shilla MyungBoRang Silver Crafts*

KIM Miyoun

김미연 (金美延) KIM Miyoun.
Peony. Wedding box. 2015. Fine
silver, fine-silver wire, enamel. 16"
× 26" × 18".

KIM Jaeyoung

김재영 (金載瑛) KIM Jaeyoung.
Bynyeo. Hairpin wedding gift (*yemul*).
Keum-boo. 24K gold, fine silver. 7".

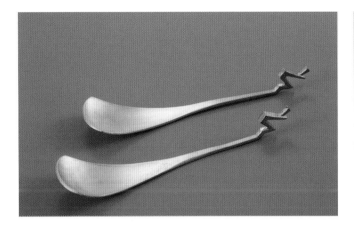

최현칠 (崔鉉七) CHOI Hyunchil. *Desert Couple Spoon Sets.* Couple set. 1990. *Keum-boo.* Sterling silver, 24K gold. 5.2" each.

최현칠 (崔鉉七) CHOI Hyunchil. *Five Various Spoons.* 1990. *Keum-boo.* Silver, 24K gold. 5.2" each.

최현칠 (崔鉉七) CHOI Hyunchil. *Wedding Crown.* Crown. 1987. Representing couple (two birds) uniting, spreading wings high and wide like a heart shape. Korean symbols of wedding jewels of corals, pearls, and diamonds are used. Sterling silver, 18K gold, diamonds, coral, pearl. 5.68" × 3.2" × 5.68".

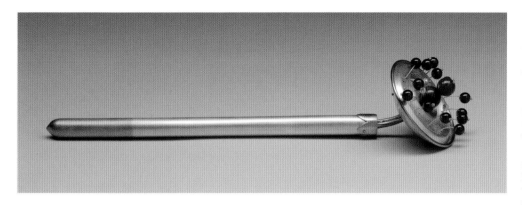

손계연 (孫係蓮) SON Kye-Yeon. *Binyeo.* Wedding hair ornament. 2007. 24K gold overlay (*keum-boo*). Fine and sterling silver, 24K gold, gold-filled wire, garnet, pearl, lapis lazuli, coral. 1.25" × 7.75" × 1.75".

Binyeo is a traditional Korean hair pin for the braided bun worn low on the neck to signify that the woman is married. This piece uses *keum-boo* techniques with 24K gold for its symbolic value, and blue and red beads, which reflect the traditional wedding colors, while garnet beads and pearls are added as a symbol of fertility.

JOO Sowon

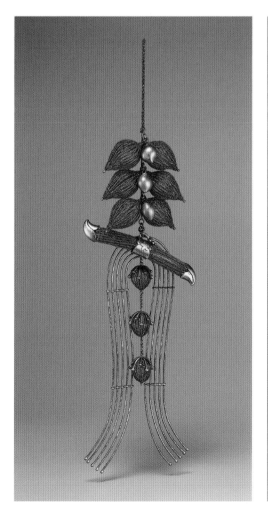

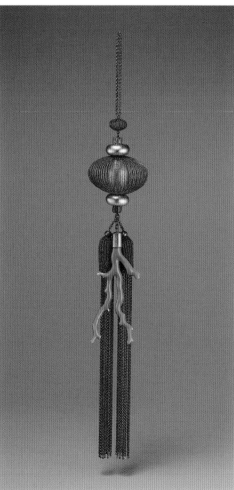

주소원 (朱昭媛) JOO Sowon. *Norigae with Ornamental Silver Knife.* Korean traditional ornament/ jewelry for *hanbok.* Wedding gift (*yemul*). 2017. This *norigae* has symbols of the peach and chili peppers. These represent the blessing of many children and prosperous families. Sterling silver (oxidized), 24K gold leaf, coral, and crochet with fine silver wire instead of traditional silk thread macramé. 18" × 4" × 1.5".

Norigae is a decorative ornament for the Korean traditional costume, *hanbok.* It usually consists of the main ornament, knots, and tassels. It is considered a good-luck charm and has been worn as a fashion accessory.

주소원 (朱昭媛) JOO Sowon. *Norigae with Ornamental Silver Knife.* Korean traditional ornament/ jewelry for *hanbok.* Wedding gift (*yemul*). 2017. This *norigae* has symbols of coral branches (wealth). Sterling silver (oxidized), 24K gold leaf, coral branch, and silver wire crochet. 18" × 4" × 2".

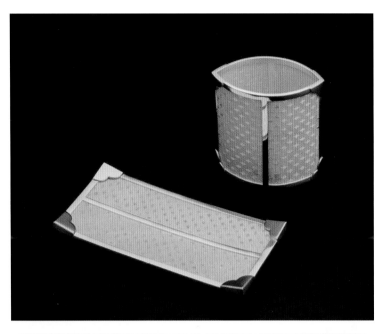

홍경희 (洪京姬) HONG Kyung Hee. *Happy Announcement*. Platter and pen-holding container. 1988. Hand weaving, fabricating, constructing, and finishing. 24K gold, fine and sterling silver. 0.9" × 7.4" × 3.6"; 4.1" × 3.9" × 2.4".

Many works are produced with a combination of specific precious metals and weaving techniques because of their symbolic meaning for the newlywed couple. Jade, coral, amber, butterflies, and bats hold wedding symbolism.

홍경희 (洪京姬) HONG Kyung Hee. *Wedding Toast*. Wedding goblet. 1988. Weaving, raising, forming, constructing, gold plating, and assembling finish. Fine and sterling silver, gold plating. 12.4" × 5.3" × 5.3".

김재영 (金載瑛) KIM Jaeyoung.
Hexagonal Coronet for Wedding Crown. Crown wedding gift (*yemul*). 1984. Silver crown, punched-out patterns accentuated with meaningful everlasting longevity, happiness and luck, on large 24K gold *keum-boo*-shaped patterns. 24K gold, fine silver, sapphire. 3.2" × 4" × 4".
Collection of Sookmyung Women's University Museum

The 24K gold twisted wires connect hanging movable blue beads. When the bride walks in during the wedding march, the dangling ornamental jewels accentuate her movements.

김재영 (金載瑛) KIM Jaeyoung.
Nine Section Container. Container with lid. 1984. Forming, constructing, chasing and repoussé patterns (*tachul*), and 24K gold overlay patterns (*keum-boo*). Fine and sterling silver, 24K gold. 4" × 12" × 12".

This container has nine sections for storing dried appetizers. This container has the traditional motifs of chrysanthemum flower patterns and Chinese characters that designate long life. It is often given as a wedding gift.

김재영 (金載瑛) KIM Jaeyoung.
Sugar & Creamer Set on the Wooden Tray. Wedding gift (*yemul*). 2004. 5.67" × 13.6" × 3.8".

Silver bowls were created by scoring and bending methods similar to paper folding and were soldered with upside-down V shapes with 24K gold (*keum-boo*) on the corners of each bend. The knob handles are 24K-gold-plated ducks (which symbolize happiness) facing each other. The walnut wooden tray symbolizes happiness. This set is displayed with silver spoons and chopsticks set with 24K gold pattern decorations (*keum-boo*) at the end of the handles.

김승희 (金昇姬) KIM Seung Hee.
Jade Wedding Box 1. Jewel
container wedding gift (*yemul*).
1980. Fabricated, assembled,
riveted, hinged finish for the
wedding rituals. *Chuncheon* jade,
sterling silver. 1.5" × 4" × 4".

Jade is important for many
reasons in Korea, especially
chuncheon jade, which is believed
to bring health and prosperity.
Therefore, using this jade is
especially important in relation to
wedding events.

김미연 (金美延) KIM Miyoun.
Happy Day. Container wedding gift
(*yemul*). 2006. Mitering, hinging,
fabricating, enameling with cloisonné
finish (*seon chilbo*). Enamel, fine
silver. 1.3" × 3.5" × 1.9" each.

Korean-to-English Glossary

장석 *jangseok*: Joinery

선상감 *seon ssanggum* (끼움 입사 *kkium ipsa*): Line inlay

점입사 *jeom ipsa*: Dot inlay

포목상감 *poamock ssanggum* (쪼음입사 *jjoeum ipsa)*: Korean damascene (Cloth inlay)

오동상감 *odong ssanggum* (*ipsa*): Black-crow color inlay (copper with 7–10 percent gold)

절상감 *jeoul ssanggum* (*ipsa*): Marriage of metals

쪼이상감 *jjoi ssanggum* (*ipsa*): Hammer-chasing-engraving technique

누금 *nugeum*: Granulation. Also referred to as *nukeum*.

금부 *keum-boo*: 24K gold overlay on silver. Also referred to as *kum-bu* or *geumbu*.

금박 *keumbak*: 24K gold leaf overlay. Also referred to as *geumpak*.

타출 *tachul*: Chasing and repoussé

옻칠 *ottchil*: Lacquering with sumac sap

나전(자개)칠 *najeon jagaechil*: Mother-of-pearl overlay on Korean lacquer

나전칠기 *najeon chilgi:* container with *najeon jagaechil*

칠보 *chilbo*: Enameling

돌입사 *dohl seokhwe ipsa*: Stone-crushed cold inlay

옥공예 *ok gong-ye*: Jade crafts

홀래 *hollye*: Wedding ceremony

예물 *yemul*: Wedding gift

비녀 *binyeo*: Hair stick on the back chignon among married women

노리개 *norigae*: Pendant with Korean macramé tassel hanging

장도 *jangdo*: Hand knife (pocketknife size) for women's emergency protection

쌍가락지 *ssang-garackgii*: Double wedding ring

침통 노리개 *chimtong norigae*: Acupuncture norigae ornament

비치모 *bichimo*: Kingfisher feathers used to embellish crafts

홍파리 *hongparii*: Red glass jewel

청파리 *chongparii*: Blue glass jewel

한복 *hanbok*: Korean traditional wear (outfits)

저고리 *jeoguri*: Upper part of traditional Korean women's garment

치마 *chima*: Traditional Korean women's skirt

색동 *saekdong*: The colorful rainbow stripes that can be seen on Korean traditional garment's sleeves, for children and women

열소| *yeolswe*: Lock with key. Also referred to as *jamulswe*.

떨잠 *ddeoljam*: Trembling/fluttering hair ornament

Bibliography

2015 Exhibition of Works by Holders of Important Intangible Cultural Heritages. *Beautiful Living*, September 18, 2005, Doosung Press.

"A Study of Art Jewelry Based on Filigree Technique—Focusing on Study of 'Hair.'" MFA thesis research paper, Kookmin University, Department of Metal Craft, 2011.

Art Collections of the Sookmyung Women's University Museum, February 20, 1993. No. 3-52 (1968, 3.20).

Buyeo National Museum. Seoul, Korea: Ahn Graphics, December 20, 2011.

Choi, Ungchang. *IPSA: Design Resource Book No. 11*. Seoul, Korea: Korean Crafts & Design Foundation, 2016.

Choi, Ung-Cheon, and Yeon-Soo Kim. *Metal Craft*. Rediscovered Beauty of Korean Metalcraft 8. December 20, 2003.

Choi, Ung-Cheon, Lee Kui-Young, and Kyung-Eun Park. *Korean Metal Craft: The Brilliant & Exquisite Beauty*. Seoul, Korea: National Museum of Korea, Tongcheon Muhwasa Printing, June 20, 1978.

Exquisite and Precious: The Splendor of Korean Art. Leeum Samsung Museum of Art, Poori Design, July 2, 2015.

The Glory of Korean Inlaid Metal Arts. Special Exhibition '97, National Museum of Korea, Seoul, July 7, 1997.

The Golden Arts of Silla. 2001 Special Traveling Exhibition, 2001 City Partner.

Hong Jungsil. *Korean Metalcraft Tools*. January 20, 1998.

Hong Jungsil. *The Spirit of Craftsmanship and Techniques*. Guil-Guem Metal Arts Research Center, Yaemek Print Tach December 15, 2006.

Hong Jungsil. *Culture of Black Iron*. Guil-Guem Metal Arts Research Center, December 23, 2008.

The Inaugural Exhibition Catalogue of the Pudeok Memorial Gallery 1999. Ewha Womans University Museum, May 31, 1999, Seoul, Korea: Ewha Womans University Press, 1999.

Ipsa Craft: The Glory of Inlay Metal Arts. Special exhibition to celebrate Year of Korean Heritage & Culture, National Museum of Korea, July 7, 1997. Seoul, Korea: National Museum of Korea, 1997.

Jangseok: The Korean Traditional Metal Work for Joinery; Korean Craft & Design Resource Book 2004. National Important Intangible Cultural Property No. 64: Kim Guk Cheon and Park Mun Yeol. Seoul, Korea: Korean Craft & Design Foundation, December 20, 2003.

Jung Young Kuwan. "Granulation & Filigree: Based on Arm Bracelet." MFA thesis research paper, Hongik University, June 30, 1986.

Kim Cheoul-Joo, Master Jogakjang Craftsman. Special one-person invitational exhibition of National Important Intangible Cultural Property No. 35. Sponsored by the Korean Culture & Heritage Foundation, December 3, 2007.

Kim, Myunghee. *Norigae, Joseon Dynasty Women's Pendant, Bona Museum Collection*. Seoul, Korea: Bona Museum, September 30, 2006.

Kim Sung-soo. *Ottchil: Beyond Millennium and the Great World of Ottchil Art* (Korean lacquer art). Seoul, Korea: Nanok, May 10, 2013.

Kim Yong-Woon, Ipsa Inlay Exhibition, Daegu Important Intangible Cultural Property No. 13, Korea Kiheok, Kim Yong-Woon, July 23, 1995.

Kwan Hang-Ah. "A Study of Ipsa Inlay Accessories Used on the Horse in the Three Kingdom Period." Special Paper 16, Dong-A University Museum, March 2003.

Kwan Hang-Ah. "The Practice and Preservation of Amalgam-Guiding." Research paper, special article of Korean Culture & Heritage, Kyeungsung University, Busan, Korea, December 2003.

Kwan Sang-ho. *Najeon Ottchil Craft* (Korean lacquer). April 20, 2007. Daewon-sa.

Kwon Hyang-Ah. "A Study on the Filigree Techniques of Earrings in the Three Kingdom Periods." Research paper, Kyungsung University, Busan, Korea, 2001.

Kwon Hyang-Ah. "A Study on the Manufacturing Techniques of Silla Earrings in the Three-Kingdoms Period." PhD diss., Dong-A University, Busan, Korea, December 2002.

Lee Hansang, ed. *Gold Crowns of Silla: Treasures from a Brilliant Age*. Translated by Junghee Lee. Seoul, Korea: Korea Foundation, 2010.

Lee Kyung Ja. *Norigae: Splendor of the Korean Costume.* Translated by Lee Jean Young. Seoul, Korea: Ewha Womans University Press, 2005.

Lee, Soyoung, and Denise Patry Leidy. *Silla: Korea's Golden Kingdom.* New York: Metropolitan Museum of Art, 2013.

Lee Yongjin. "Special Feature: Delicacy: A Close Look at *Ipsa* Wire Inlay Techniques." *National Museum of Korea* 31 (Spring 2015): 2–9.

McCreight, Tim, ed. *Metals Technic: A Collection of Techniques for Metalsmiths.* 2nd ed. Cape Elizabeth, ME: Brynmorgan, 1992.

National Palace, Museum of Korea. *The Costume of Imperial Prince Yeong Family.* Seoul, Korea: Yaemek, June 23, 2010.

Oh Sun Hee. "A Study on Women's Binyeo (Hairpin) in Joseon Period." MA thesis research paper, Department of Clothing & Textiles, Ewha Womans University, January 2008.

Opulence: Treasure of Korean Traditional Craft. Root Resign, Samsung Leeum Museum of Art, Traveling Exhibition in Korea & USA, Catalog, March 28, 2013.

Personal Ornaments of the Joseon Dynasty. Seoul, Korea: Sookmyung Women's University Museum, 2005.

Portal, Jane, with Suhyung Kim and Hee Jung Lee. *Arts of Korea.* Boston: MFA Publications, Museum of Fine Arts, 2012.

Special Issue: Metal Crafts of Baekje and Silla. Journal of Korean Art & Archaeology 8 (2014).

Tongcheon Moonhwa-sa. *Looking into Gongju National Museum.* Seoul, Korea: National Museum, January 2011.

Yi Young-Hoon, Yoon On-Sik, Soyoung Lee, and Denise Patry Leidy. "Gyeongju National Museum: Cultural Treasures of the Silla Kingdom." *Arts of Asia* 43, no. 5 (September–October 2013): 63–105.

Yoo Bong Ja. "A Study on the Jewelry Using the Inlaid Technology." PhD diss., Department of Metal Crafts, Daegu Catholic University, February 2010.

Index